THE BEGGARS' BROTHERHOOD

By the same author

Literary Craftsmanship and Appreciation

La. Crown 8vo.   *8s. 6d. net.*

This book discusses and links together the craft of
writing and the creative art of reading. It falls thus into
two main divisions. There is, in the first part, an intro-
duction on the use of the imagination, followed by
chapters on description, humour, and the writing of
letters, fiction, verse, etc. The remaining part of the
book deals with such themes as the nature and appre-
ciation of poetry and the reading of literature. It ap-
proaches the subject both from the point of view of
the apprentice who is learning his job and of the
schoolmaster who is trying to teach it.

AN UPRIGHT MAN

THE BEGGARS' BROTHERHOOD

by

RONALD FULLER

LONDON
GEORGE ALLEN & UNWIN LTD
MUSEUM STREET

FIRST PUBLISHED IN 1936

TO E. W. BLIGH

IN

GENIAL MEMORY

OF

"The *Sun,* the *Dog,* the triple *Tunne*"

CONTENTS

PAGE

BEGINNING   13

PART ONE

THE BROTHERHOOD OF BEGGARS

I.   MEDIAEVAL BEGGARS   19
II.   THE CAUSES OF THE BROTHERHOOD   27
III.   THE WAR ON THE BEGGARS   40
IV.   THE BEGGARS   56
V.   THE BROTHERHOOD   86
VI.   NOTABLE BEGGARS   100

PART TWO

THE FRATERNITY OF CONEY-CATCHERS

VII.   ELIZABETHAN LONDON   117
VIII.   ROBERT GREENE   136
IX.   THE NIP AND THE FOIST   146
X.   THE LAWS OF THE CONEY-CATCHERS   165
XI.   THE ROARING BOYS   177

PART THREE

THE DECLINE OF THE BROTHERHOODS

XII.   THE LAST OF THE BEGGARS   191
XIII.   THE HIGHWAYMEN   201
XIV.   THE LAST OF THE CONEY-CATCHERS   221
    ENDING   241
    INDEX   245

LIST OF ILLUSTRATIONS

I. AN UPRIGHT MAN   *frontispiece*
(*From an old print*)

II. THE COUNTERFEIT CRIPPLE   41
(*From Barclay's Ship of Folys, 1570*)

III. THE SCOURGE AND THE PILLORY   51
(*From the Bagford Ballads*)

IV. BAMPFYLDE-MOORE CAREW, KING OF
     THE BEGGARS   *facing page* 56
(*From an old print*)

V. TITLE-PAGE TO COPLANDE'S PAMPHLET   63
(*From the edition of 1531*)

VI. NICHOLAS GENINGS AS AN UPRIGHT MAN
     AND A COUNTERFEIT CRANK   69
(*From Harman's Caveat, 1566*)

VII. MAD TOM OF BEDLAM   80
(*From the Bagford Ballads*)

VIII. LONG MEG OF WESTMINSTER   111
(*From the Whole Life and Death of Long Meg, 1582*)

IX. SAINT PAUL'S AND THE RIVER   *facing page* 118
(*From A. van der Wyngaerde's Panorama, 1543*)

X. ROBERT GREENE   144
(*From Dickenson's Greene in Conceipt new Raised from the Grave, 1598*)

XI. TAVERN FROLLICK   *facing page* 146
(*From the English Rogue, 1668*)

XII. MOLL FRITH   ,,   176
(*From Middleton's Roaring Girle, 1611*)

XIII. ROARING BOYS   181
(*From the Bagford Ballads*)

XIV. MAUNDERERS ON THE PAD   *facing page* 202
(*From the English Rogue, 1668*)

XV. DICK SWIFT   ,,   220
(*From an old print*)

XVI. TAILPIECE   243
(*From the Bagford Ballads*)

BEGINNING

I wish I could think that Nostalgia meant the grief of the νοΰς—Mind's Woe. It is a lovely word; and would describe well enough our queer homesickness for dead history, and the way we sentimentalize over fleeting and forgotten things. We look back with curious eyes upon the past, always seeking and forever failing to relate it completely to the present. For no sooner do events and personalities fade into that dim Backward than they change also. The villains of the Middle Ages have become romantic to the twentieth century, however monstrous they may have appeared to the fourteenth. The sordid is transformed to the picturesque; the mean, the disreputable and the hideous are all woven about by the transmuting alchemy of age. We cannot hate forgotten evil, any more than we can hate Mr. Pecksniff or Iago. Looking down on them from our great heights and infinite distances, we cannot convince ourselves that they are walking still about our living world.

I suppose it is because of this that the pirates, the most horrible collection of ruffians that ever poisoned the seas, are as heroic to us as they were hateful to their contemporaries: and we love to think upon such dark rogues as Captain Avery or Blackbeard striding their bloodstained decks or dangling in tarred chains by Wapping Old Stairs. It is for this reason, too, that a certain glamour surrounds those thousands of highwaymen, beggars and cheats that walked three centuries ago the roads of England.

For we are further removed than by a mere three hundred years from the age of Shakespeare. We are creatures of another planet. Since the days of Nicholas Genings and his rowsy rabblement, the whole face of England has altered. The country has, like the tramp, become romantic largely because, like the tramp, it has almost disappeared. In a time when men were more accustomed to walking than riding, to use one's legs was no very glamorous occupation. But to us the wandering picklocks and pedlars who mumped down their green lanes have become invested with the romantic aura of hardihood, liberty and courage. That Escapism which sends us into the country at week-ends sends us searching through history for a glimpse of freer and more spacious times. We envy and admire the liberty of the beggar or the gypsy because we are ourselves in chains; and to us Autolycus was always merrily tramping the footpath-way, singing in the summer fields. To the Elizabethans he was a very real menace; he was one of an increasing and dangerous brotherhood of thieves, a desperate outcast preying on the fopperies of the world.

Hypocrisy, shamelessness and quick cunning are the talents of the tramp; dirt and destitution his inevitable lot. And whatever fantasies we may weave about singing stalwarts picking the berries at the wayside and waving their beer-mugs under the moon, these rogues, as we more curiously examine them, become stuff of the earth and no heroes for sentimental balladry. However much we may enjoy from a discreet distance the contemplation of knavery, our narrower scrutiny brings disillusion. The Eliza-bethan tramp was a bestial creature, living in circumstances of appalling squalor; the seven deadly Sinnes slept in his Pocket, and he never drew money but the noyse awoke them. . . . But the Elizabethan tramp has departed, and with him has departed also the legion of gulls and conies which was his excellent prey. His villainies have faded with time. The "Trumpet of Antiquitie giveth a very uncertain sound"; and history has but a shadowy remembrance of dark taverns where money passed at midnight, of stealthy gangs lurking in back-streets, of sun-burned, ruthless men listening at the lane's end for the clatter of approaching hoofs.

PART ONE

THE BROTHERHOOD OF BEGGARS

I

MEDIAEVAL BEGGARS

I⊤ was not for nothing that the Elizabethans divided society into wolves and rabbits, the Coney-catcher and the Coney—

> Man's life's a Play, the Worlde's a Stage, whereon
> Learn thou to Play—or else be Played upon.

Even if their ancient trade has fallen into disrepute, every nation is a nation of vagabonds grown respectable.

Vagabondage, after all, is a not unnatural instinct— the instinct to have done with responsibility and the conventions, the instinct to live like a gentleman without having to work like a navvy. There is something pleasantly childlike about the elemental desire for adventure. But the older one grows the less ambitious one becomes. In its cradle a child may want to play with the moon, like a great golden guinea; in its sober dotage it is content to play with the guineas and leave the moon alone. But tramps really do want to play with the moon; for the wind and the stars are their companions and the canopy of the sky the only roof that gives them shelter in their cities of kites and crows. In the Elizabethan age the gypsies were called the "Moon Men." The mystery of their origin is still unsolved; and it occurs to me that they really might have been blown by some incalculable wind from that icy and virginal planet.

There is something to be said for the sentimental

attitude I am, at the moment, adopting. Unaccommo-
dated man is no more but such a poor, bare, forked
animal : and the desire that Dekker expressed through
the mouth of his vagabond orator is one that has been
felt by man since the days of Petronius. "Doe we not
all come into the Worlde," he cries in his drunken
peroration, "like arrant Beggars, without a rag upon
us? Doe we not all go out of the Worlde like Beggars,
saving an old sheete to cover us? And shall we not all
walke up and downe in the Worlde like Beggars, with
an old Blankett pinned about us?"

The story of the tramp is as ancient as the story
of mankind; but the Brotherhood of Beggars is of
more recent growth, the evidence for which is found
in one particular branch of literature. A thing is
never written about till it becomes big enough or
dangerous enough to be noticed : and tramps did not
attract the alarmed attention of literary men till the
sixteenth century. The golden age of the tramp was
from 1530 till 1630. They appeared suddenly like a
portent. By the end of the century they had swollen
to a great army led by a king and his officers, and ruled
by a series of complicated laws. Their decline was
gradual but inevitable throughout the seventeenth
century : and after 1630, though the beggars remained
in thousands, the Beggars' Brotherhood had disappeared for good.

There had been gangs of vagabonds often enough
in the Middle Ages. The very word "robber" has
been ingeniously and erroneously derived from the
"Roberdes knaves" in *Piers Plowman,* a gang of
murderers and "draw-latches" of the fourteenth
century, composed chiefly of masterless villeins or

landless men in search of employment. The drawlatch
was later known as a picklock. The writer of one of
those enormous theological treatises which tower
like ruined and formidable monoliths along the paths
of mediaeval literature, describes them exactly as
their successors were to appear to the Elizabethans.
If the thieves were unlucky enough to find the owner
in, they would spin him a piteous tale about the burning
of their house and the loss of all their goods. Sometimes
they would claim that they were once rich men, "&
now thei haue ryzt nouzt"; or that they had lost
"hors & harneys" beyond the sea. But if only the
woman of the house were in, they would force an
entry and demand compassion with threats.[1]

"Danyel the dees-pleyere and Denote the baude
(or drawlatch) and frere the faitour"—the shamming
beggar—were among that sad little group denied the
pity of Piers Plowman;[2] and feeling ran high against
them in the fourteenth century. A statute of Edward
III was aimed at the drawlatches. For a time they
terrorized the people of the district, and may have
been the far origin of the legends of Robin Hood's
"merry men." But these and their like were small
transitory associations of desperate men. Nor can
the random baronial sorties in search of plunder or
excitement be called in any sense fraternities. Many
of these barons lived in huge manors strong as castles,
and surrounded by regiments of armed retainers,
willing enough to become highwaymen, raiders or
kidnappers at the wish of their master. Such was Sir
Gosseline Deuville in the reign of Edward II. But a

---

[1] *Jacob's Well*, E.E.T.S. (O.S. 115), I, pp. 134–135.
[2] *Piers Plowman*, ed. T. Wright, I, p. 121.

hundred and fifty years earlier, in the London of Henry II, lived a dim, sinister figure named William Longbeard, who plotted villainy against kings like a Borgia, "stroaking his long beard which he curiously fostered." Longbeard had at his back a company of genuine tramps, tattered and depraved, and headed processions through the streets of the town "as if he had been the proude Changuis leading his legions of Tartars thorow Europe."[1] I like to think of him as the first of the Beggar Kings who became in later days so numerous: and certainly his downfall was as picturesque as his career. He was brought to bay at last by the royal troops in a Cheapside carpenter's shop, where he laid about him lustily with his axe, giving his men time to find sanctuary in Bow Church. There he joined them hotly pursued. Longbeard and his rabble stoutly defended the Church, till they were smoked out by burning straw to die in the streets.

These forerunners of the beggars and the Coney-catchers, the romantic robbers of the Middle Ages, were isolated figures. The tales of Reynard the Fox at the court of Nobel are the earliest Coney-catching pamphlets, and the stories of how he beats Lampe the virtuous rabbit, sets traps for Isegrim, and hoists the simple Bruin with his own petard are duplicated a hundred times in the later journalistic excursions of the Elizabethans. There were stories of semi-mythical gangsters, remote, heroic creatures like George a Greene and Robert the Devil, whose ghastly career was largely spent in killing hermits, torturing cats and stabbing pedagogues. There were huge and shadowy figures who loom through the mists of endless legends.

[1] Lodge, *Life and Death of William Longbeard,* 1593, p. 32.

A certain Rugosa was said to have been the Adam of the Beggars' Brotherhood, till "the doctor of the triple tree applied the powerful cordial of Hemp":[1] but nothing except his traditional end has survived. All these tales of impossible heroes and villains satisfied the mediaeval love of the marvellous and their insatiable demand for tall stories. Side by side with the deeds of Tom of Lincoln and Guy of Warwick were the crude practical jokes of Howleglass and Scogan, told and retold in a million "merrie tales." Beggars were common enough, and Chaucer alone is evidence for the existence of the fourteenth-century Coney-catcher. But beggary had not yet become a trade of shame. Beggary only becomes disgraceful when a population increases. In primitive and sparsely populated lands it is a wholly natural way of living. The mediaeval knight-errant would have been hauled off to gaol as a sturdy rogue by the Elizabethans. For all his fights with giants, his sojourn in the Castle of Adamant, his passage of the Gulf Perilous, Huon of Bordeaux is a man of no fixed abode and no certain employment; the favourite prey of the Headborough. The golden age of the wanderer, the hiker, was the fourteenth century: of the tramp, the sixteenth. Between 1300 and 1400 the roads were crowded with Chaucerian pilgrims, on their way to shrines, universities or markets. There were roaming pedlars, Reliquaries, pardoners, degenerate friars and vagrant scholars, most of whom were killed off later during the reformation. There were thousands of quacks, astrologers, palmists: rogues like Albumazar Meteoroscopico in the old

---

[1] John Shirley, *Triumph of Wit*, 1724, p. 143.

play, or that plausible knave Doctor Pinchbacke, who exploited the unfailing gullibility of mankind. He had begun as a plain cozener, cheating stray countryfolk at cards in the market square; but, finding all his shifts worn threadbare, he adopted the alias of Pinchbacke and put up at a tavern. He established his reputation for wizardry by stealing a goblet and then suggesting to the distracted landlord that, for forty shillings, he could "cast a figure" and recover it. After a month of free lodging his art enabled him to discover the goblet at the bottom of a well, and with a substantial reward and the beginnings of a reputation he set out on his travels. He was eventually hanged at Exeter for a murder which he did not commit: a pleasant instance of poetic justice.

The Astrologer did not disappear for many years, and it was against this type of Coney-catcher that Reginald Scot wrote parts of his *Discoverie of Witchcraft.* This did for Divination what Greene's pamphlets did for cheats of a less mystical order. As late as 1590 Chettle describes Doctor Pinchbacke's trick performed by another knave of the same kind, who caused his servant to hide a great silver salt cellar under his capouch and to cast it secretly into a filthy pond. The owners of the salt cellar flocked to the Astrologer, imploring him to use his sinister arts. For what he called a trifling consideration he agreed to help them and after grave consultation with the stars directed them to the pond. Thus the whole town was full of the cunning of the man, "that indeed," comments the writer, "had only conny-catcht his host."

The tramps remained: but there was a very real difference between the tramps of the Middle Ages and the tramps of the Renaissance. In the Middle Ages a tramp was something of a hero. He was usually an outlaw, like the Pinner of Wakefield. He lived with a few trusty followers under the greenwood tree, and, as long as the fine weather lasted, was romantic in a mild sort of way, like the hero of the *Nut-brown Maid*. When he died he swung in chains from a tall tree, frightening travellers in the moonlight, keeping ward over his phantasmal sheep. At his feet the forked mandrake, born from his blood, lay in wait for hungry but unwary pedestrians. England in those days was a great green marsh, relieved here and there by forests. And as long as the outlaw kept to the woods he was a romantic and exciting figure, a children's bogey, like the Black Douglas. It was when he was landed in a mediaeval dungeon, some fetid, toad-ridden place where limbs rotted off, that his life began to lose its glamour. The mediaeval tramp was like a wild beast and lived in the forest, with occasional unpremeditated visits to the town. But the Elizabethan tramp lived in the town and only retired to the desolate country when the town became too hot to hold him. Mediaeval tramps were isolated: they never formed themselves into a band—except once, when they marched in a frowning body to Smithfield, and were laughed at by a boy. The only brotherhood of beggars in the Middle Ages was of men who had wedded themselves to poverty, brothers alike of birds and beggars, the Friars of Saint Francis of Assisi. And the true difference between the beggars of the Middle Ages and the beggars of the sixteenth century is the difference between the outlaw and the fraternity. The mediaeval tramp lived alone in forest and swamp. The Elizabethan tramp sang and made merry and fashioned his counterfeit sores with his ragged fellows amid the taverns of Whitefriars and the drains of Moorditch.

II

THE CAUSES OF THE BROTHERHOOD

THE decline of an individual or an institution is often more crowded with incident than the period of its prosperity. The decay of the body politic is as full of hideous activity as the decay of any other body: and there must elapse a long period of disaster and suffering before the Phoenix can arise from the worm that its own ashes have engendered.

For a hundred years of confusion and chaos the Middle Ages lingered on its death-bed. The symptoms of the emergence of the new state appeared simultaneously with the symptoms of the disappearance of the old; but among the many things which changed and decayed, and yet did not wholly disappear, was the Tramp.

The sudden increase and most uproarious fruition of beggardom was, like the spots on a diseased skin, one of the symptoms of the perishing of the Middle Ages. The first occasion on which there was anything like an organized association of beggars banded together for a common purpose was when, in 1481, the men of Kent followed Walter Tyler, "the enraged boor," as the chronicler calls him, to beard the nobles at Smithfield. Providence by means of the Black Death and peasants with the aid of pitchforks together succeeded in altering the old order beyond report, thought or belief. By the end of the fifteenth century landlords were no longer employing platoons of inarticulate Gurths, branded to servitude like sheep, but were beginning to rent out their lands to small farmers. These in their turn employed free labour when they could get it, and paid high enough wages, till the devastation of the Black Death had been forgotten. The villeins were freed: their irons were knocked off: they scattered over the country to become farmers themselves, to drift into the great towns as craftsmen, to wield a pike in the Low Countries or to stand behind the guns of the Armada. When, at the close of the fifteenth century, there came a sudden drop in wages, numbers of them took to the roads, padding the haphazard hoof from day to day; a helpless crowd, and harmless—so long as they remained disunited and unorganized. The tiny seed of professional vagabondage which was to sprout into so rich and monstrous a blossom was sown in the Plague; and thereafter the roads became more and more thickly thronged with wayfarers more and more dubious, till anyone who expressed a wish to leave his native village and "travel" had to obtain a permit and explain his ambitions more particularly. The Town Seal together with a testimonial permitting them to beg within certain hundreds was given to travellers. If a "Ruffler or valiant beggar" had been whipped and sent home, he could apply to a constable for relief on the journey, for they were all given testimonials guaranteeing that they had been well and truly whipped. Even University students, hiking back to keep a term at Oxford or Cambridge and systematically begging from house to house, had to possess their permits with the signature of the Chancellor.

Unemployment, "the mother and breeder of Vacaboundes," paralysed the country during the early part of the sixteenth century. Many beggars who later swelled the ranks of the Brotherhood had grown up all their days in vagabondage. The poverty of the lower classes even at the very end of the century was appalling. Children of poor folk "beginne to shifte and acquaint themselves with some one like brought uppe, that hath made his shifte, with dicyng, cosenynge, picking or cutting of purses, or els if he be of courage plaine robbing by the waie side . . . & so come they daily to the gallowes."[1] They or their fathers had once been the retainers of great barons, whom the growing evil of Maintenance had turned into a crude kind of highway robber. Some of them had belonged to the companies of wandering outlaws that had either fleeted the time carelessly in the greenwood or sold their unscrupulous services to some neighbouring baron.

The existence of these barons had prevented anything like a tramps' brotherhood in the Middle Ages. But the barons had destroyed themselves in a series of fatal and futile battles; and their mercenaries, obscurely and with appalling speed, gathered to maunder along the highways. Piers Penniless was no more the pitiful isolated figure he had been in the days of Langland and Chaucer; he was becoming the malevolent and menacing tatterdemalion with whom Elizabethan nursemaids used to cow their refractory charges.

The enclosure of arable land for pasture recruited an enormous number for the ragged regiments. Woeful experience showed how it unhoused hundreds

[1] R. Hitchcocke, *A Pollitique Platt*, 1580, Sig. E1. r.

who begged or stole for a living, till desperate need
thrust them on the gallows. Sheep-farming meant,
of course, that a few shepherds lived in the ruins of
what had once been a prosperous village. Writers
of the time complained bitterly enough that sheep
were becoming devourers of men, a sinister reversal
of the natural order. "They consume, destroye and
devoure whole fieldes, howses and cities," said Sir
Thomas More. The evicted ploughman, finding no
employment where once the land had supported
him and a hundred more, trudged off along the muddy
roads with wife and children at his heels. And finally,
"what can they then els doo but steale, and then
justly (pardy!) be hanged, or els go about beggynge?"[1]
In one of the many dialogues published in the sixteenth century a Husbandman complains that he
has known a dozen ploughs abandoned within less
compasse than sixe myles. The trouble was not that
the enclosure of land was in itself a disaster; indeed,
"wise old Fuller" is at pains to point out how useful
hedges would be to take cover behind in the event
of a foreign invasion, where they would "serve for
barracadoes, and stick as birdlime in the wings of
the horse, and scotch the wheeling about of the foot."[2]
It was that the attitude of rich men towards the land
was changing. For the first time the peculiar idea
occurred to them that land might be exploited as a
personal possession. The phantoms of a million
notices to trespassers stood shadowy by a million
woods. In an eloquent, sincere, but rather cloudy
sermon Robert Crowley commented on the more than

---

[1] Sir Thomas More, *Utopia*, Bohn, I, p. 39.
[2] Thomas Fuller, *Holy and Profane State*, 1648, II, xiii.

Turkish behaviour of these oppressive landlords.
The Lord would forbid the clouds of his mercy to
rain upon their intolerable heads with the sweet
dew of his grace; and he claims with a kind
of bewildered anger that the whole earth, by
birthright, "belongeth to the children of men.
They are all inheritours thereof indifferently by
nature."

But the idea that land could be jealously protected
and used as a supply for general rather than individual
demand was to the capitalist an exciting thought; and
during the rush to make a corner in this new com-
modity there was (as is usual on such occasions)
little generosity shown to the evicted peasants. "A
few rich cobs get into their clutches almost whole
countries so as the poore can have no releefe by them,"
complains Stubbes. "For by this meanes pastures
and groundes are not only excessively deere, but also
not to be had of anie poore man for money." They
could not even keep a cow; the open moors and
commons where, since the days of the Conqueror,
the poor man's cattle had grazed were taken from him
to become "private property," and the wretched
peasants were compelled either to beg or starve.
Rents towered to incredible heights. Even though a
man had been for years an honest tenant, yet he
had either to buy his land immediately or, as Crowley
put it, "void in haste." Pamphlets of the period
contain pitiful accounts of the state of the poor. No
mercy was shown. "Owt he must, be he never so
poore; though he should become a beggar, and
after a thefe, and so at length be hanged by his
owtgoing; so lytle is the lawe of love regarded, oh

cruel tyrannys!"[1] The upstart merchant class, which
was rapidly taking the place of the old nobility,
possessed none even of the magnificent failings of
their predecessors; none of the feudal arrogance
and cruel splendour of the barons. They compensated
for this lack by the possession of a typically middle-
class characteristic, an unimaginative professional
greed: the greed for possessions rather than that
greed for power which had led to the downfall of
so many of the proud families whose positions they
very successfully usurped. Harrison, in his *Description
of England*, alludes to the callousness with which the
wealthy merchant would discover some means of
evicting his tenants and turning the land they had
occupied to his private gain. Not one of them had
the smallest idea what trouble he was laying up for a
later generation.

This sudden rise of the merchant class to wealth
coincided with the discovery of the New World
where so many sturdy beggars were to end their
days, with the rapid expansion of London and the
equally rapid fall in prices. The country was like a
young man coming suddenly into an inheritance
too large for his self-control; and money was flung
right and left. The literature of the time is full of
diatribes against the extravagance of the wealthy.
This was no new thing. A very long time before
the *Parson's Tale* dress had been a favourite Aunt
Sally of the pulpit; but now the thunder of the
preacher had been borrowed by the journalist.
The gallant was the "buffoon and baboon" of the
times, a "nitid spark"; the rich lady who distorted

---

[1] *Complaynt of Roderyck Mors*, 1542, cap. ii (E.E.T.S.).

in the cause of fashion the shape God had bestowed on her was more like a Monster of Aegypt than a modest mayden of Europe. Against this extravagant display of wealth and "inordinate excess in apparrell" the Sumptuary Laws were futile. There were numberless arrests and fines. In 1571 two tailor's servants were prosecuted for the wearing of "great and monsterous briches." Eleven years later all apprentices were forbidden to wear hats in the City and ordered to dress soberly in woollen or leathern doublets and "little breeches," but the Englishman's fashions in clothes remained the butt of the satirist for many years. Nash thundered against this second daughter of Pride like an Old Testament prophet, and Stubbes has a long passage on the same theme. "Great and monsterous ruffs" the people would wear, and hats that baffled his powers of description. The poor, he adds, lay on straw pallets in the streets or died like dogs. The wealth of the upper classes was a standing temptation to the avarice of the lower; and tramps and Coney-catchers gathered about the "Gulls" like parasites on the back of some large, foolish and opulent fish.

The vast trains of servants that followed the gay arrogant youths about the streets became a fertile reinforcement to the Beggars' Brotherhood, for if the master fell ill or lost his money the servant would be turned out on the roads to starve or thieve. The old status of the serving man was rapidly changing. In the Middle Ages he had been more like a member of a private bodyguard, fighting for his master in time of war and planting cabbages for him in the intervals. But the transition was at hand to the day

c

when the servant became a sort of travelling companion to his master, as Strap was to Roderick Random or Partridge to Tom Jones or Sam Weller to Mr. Pickwick. The serving man had won a hundred battles for his masters in the thirteenth and fourteenth centuries; but his knell had sounded—

> Downe *Plumpton Parke* as I did passe,
> I heard a Bird sing in a glen:
> The cheefest of her song it was——
> Farewell, the flower of serving men!

Such was the epitaph written on them by John Musgrave, who was himself hanged for robbing the King's Retriever.

In one pamphlet dialogue of the time a Townsman named Vallentine is discussing with his friend Vincent the ancient topic, the relative merits of town and country life. Vincent, the countryman, remarks that he has a large number of servants to follow him in the streets or to "grace his hall" at home. "Lubberly Monckes and fat-headed Friers," says Vallentine, pointing out that these hosts of servants may have been very necessary during the old baronial wars, but have now become a standing army of beggars. The new class was too rich to be charitable. "You ask why cunning and cunny-catching be so common? Money, I say, Money is the cause of all this mischiefe and miserie."

In the old days charity had been as much the unquestioned duty of a gentleman as going to church was in the last century. In 1600, when a servant became too old to work, he was turned out of doors to beg away the winter of his days; but the older nobles had pensioned them as a matter of course or tradition. All kinds of odd independent and private charities died with the sixteenth century. There would come no more like Robert Chickley to order a "competent dinner" and twopence a head to be given annually to 2,400 paupers. The town bells used to ring when Master Redman, Bishop of Ely, travelled abroad: and the poor folk clustered about the wheels of his carriage for the sixpences he showered upon them. With the old days disappeared the old manners; and gone for good were the great chines of stalled beefe and the black jacks of double Beere and the long hall tables creaking with fine victuals. The pensioners of Robert Chickley and the followers of the Bishop of Ely took to the high roads, where the custom of wearing "dags" or pistols had turned loose routs of armed roguing beggars. These were swollen by a number of disbanded soldiers who found no other use for their weapons at the close of the long wars. But the end of the struggle with France saw the beginning of a new war: the two hundred years' war against the Beggars' Brotherhood.

The closing of the monasteries and the handing over of the estates to the merchant class were visible symbols of the crumbling and collapse of the Middle Ages. The end of the monasteries meant the end of the charity which, on the whole, they had dispensed largely and well; and for many years there was no organized system to take their place. At the same time a final blow was struck at the Guilds when their property too was confiscated. The Guilds, powerful and dangerous though they had become, had pensioned their members: and when the money was gone the pensioners were left destitute. Over 88,000 people were disbanded by the closing of the monasteries alone. The homeless peasants took to the roads in sombre, penniless gangs or erected makeshift dwellings on some waste common land near their old homes. These communities grew up in the shadow of poverty and crime and nurtured their frequent offspring in the hourly menace of the gallows. Riotous apprentices were already forming the nucleus of the thieves' paradise of Whitefriars; and Stubbes accuses them of being to some degree a cause of the Brotherhood, since so many beggars were "sawcie boys" of between ten and twenty years of age who had married a "prettie pussie to huggle withall" and then discovered they had not enough money for the resultant family. All the old hospitals—St. Mary Bethlehem, St. Thomas of Southwark, St. Bartholomew—were closed till the end of Henry VIII's reign, and the inmates turned loose on the streets. The land became suddenly crowded with men in one way or another dispossessed of their livelihood. It was years since the first complaints had been made of the "ydell vacabundes" who were earning money by the pretence of impotency. The sturdy lobies had trebled their numbers. The Beggars' Brotherhood had arrived. War had begun: and the Whip, the Pillory and the Gallows started on their endless work.

The origin of the Beggars' Brotherhood is unknown; and one suspects that the beggars themselves were less conscious of the power and scope of their organization than the literary men who wrote of it. The first army of beggars was said to have been gathered about the middle of the fifteenth century and to have marched with Jack Mendall's rebels on London. They were led by an arch-thief named Roberts, and took later to the woods, where they formed a band of outlaws, preying indiscriminately upon travellers. Roberts is supposed to have been the originator of the earliest laws of the Brotherhood, a list of crude precautions against the Law of the Realm.

The first to be invented was, as might be expected, the obvious stipulation that the leader was to have first share in the booty. No murder or robbery was to be committed anywhere near the wood where the gang lived; and no one should flee for shelter to this sanctuary at the head of a hue and cry. Under the general name of Roberts' men, or Roberdes, this band was supposed to have spread all over the country and to have prospered under him till his death. He was succeeded by Jenkin Cowdiddle, a man "stout of stomacke," who goes down to incredulous posterity as the author of that notable Law that "all beggars should spend all their gettings in the day past, in good Beere or Ale."[1] Jenkin, however, together with three hundred of his "tottered knaves," was killed at Tewkesbury, and the reign of a still more legendary figure began.

This was Spising, who bearded the king, murdered, robbed and "domineered about eleven years." It was Puffing Dick the Fourth who began dividing the Brotherhood into its various orders. There were the Gentlemen Robbers who would pretend to be lawyers and decayed noblemen and made great use

---

[1] Samuel Rowlands, *Martin Markall*, 1610, p. 47.

of false beards and counterfeit heads of haire. These were later known as Upright Men. The second order of thieves was the Highwayman on Foot, and he, I suppose, was transformed by insensible degrees to the Clapperdudgeon or the Ruffler. Puffing Dick was something of a Coney-catcher, too, for he first employed the Dice cosenage: but he ended early and miserably with the "pyning of the pox." Long Lawrence invented the subtle art of Crossbiting; Skelton, his successor, established a strict rule that anyone who gave way to a gust of holiday geniality and was seen to lay aside his crutches and skip or dance was to pay a fine of two dozen of Beere. It is all very pleasant and ingenious, and reminds one of the more dubious of Old Testament genealogies; but Cocke Lorell has some claim to be a historical character.

In 1511 this curious figure was said to have instituted the Quartern of Knaves—the twenty-five orders of beggars—which had been in existence in one form or another throughout the Middle Ages. He was the Solomon of these discarded people, a Justinian of the Rabble, the "thyrde persone of Englande"; and this code of regulations for hoodwinking the constabulary was the basis of all later additions. He was the head of a band of robbers in the London streets, and became a legendary monster, the most notorious knave who ever played the padder in the riotous and magnificent days of Henry VIII. He stands, a shadowy, half-unreal shape, in the twilight between history and legend, for there were few annalists to corroborate or contradict the gossip of monks and villagers or to record the growth of this secret brotherhood. Indeed, Cocke Lorell's name—"Chief Rogue" or Losel—implies that he was merely a symbol of the forces conspiring against law and order. In Tudor literature he appears often enough as a kind of beggar Robin Hood.

But whether he was a character purely imaginary, or whether there really was some reckless and truculent rogue who plagued the Tudor police, with the end of Cocke Lorell and the dawn of the sixteenth century the beggars are no longer a mysterious menace but a threat as clear as noonday, mumping in their thousands under the hedges or at the obscure corners of the streets.

III

THE WAR ON THE BEGGARS

THE armies of order were not marshalled against the beggars in force till the sixteenth century; but the growing menace of these impostors of the streets had been recognized many years earlier. The first list of rogues appeared in the German *Ratsbuch* in 1381. In 1509 the famous *Der Betler Orden* made a more acid and exhaustive survey of the Brotherhood; and nineteen years later was edited by Martin Luther as the *Liber Vagatorum*. A "pretty little book," Luther calls it; but it is a grim enough array of knaves. Luther had himself been "cheated and befooled by such tramps and liars," and it is clear that at one time various brotherhoods existed all over Europe. The Parisian *Argotiers* had a well-developed language and government of their own. Their king was the great Chosroes, who wore a uniform of coloured rags and presided over annual councils. They were eventually uprooted by being compelled, by an edict of Francis I, to clean out the city sewers.

In England the printed onslaught against the beggar came many years later, though the pulpit had, in a hundred mediaeval sermons and homilies, satirized the types for centuries. They have a place in Barclay's *Ship of Fools*, which contains a pleasant woodcut of the counterfeit cripple, so familiar a figure later to the Elizabethans, hobbling along in his rags with a bandaged foot and a great staff in his hand. His dog and his doxy accompany him, the latter taking a surreptitious swig of ale behind his back; and beside him walks his donkey with a pannier full of disfigured brats. Some of these beggars

THE COUNTERFEIT CRIPPLE

used actually to maim their own children, "manglynge their facys, and brekynge theyr bonys" to arouse compassion.[1]

The beggar crops up again amid a company of rogues in a satirical poem called *Cock Lorells Bote*,

[1] *The Ship of Fools*, ed. T. H. Jamieson, I, p. 304.

published in 1512. Those who held an oar in that mysterious vessel were Coney-catchers of every trade. There sailed Matthew Mumchance of Shooter's Hill, Christopher Catchpoll, Wat Welbelyne the gaoler of Ludgate; and queer eccentrics like Kate with the crooked foot and Annys, who "dwelled at ye sygne of ye dogges hede in ye pot." There were pedlars among the crew and costerde mongers, bere brewers, purse cutters and dyssymulynge beggers, sluttes, drabbes, Tyburne collopes, together, it would seem, with most of the population of England— those who were not Coney-catchers being Coneys. The jolly rebels sailed from dawn till sundown out on the open sea under so large a moon that the earth seemed paved with white, fading over a horizon that was the green hills of England. For they rowed in their pilgrimage from shire to shire, from Garlyke Head to Knaves' Inn; and the last seen of them was the topsail disappearing behind a wood, and the last sound heard the call of the bosun's whistle.

Simon Fish's famous pamphlet, the *Supplicacyon for the Beggers*, was less a plea for the "nedy, impotent, blinde, lame and sike" than an attack on the counterfeit holy and idell beggers of the Church. Henry VIII came and embraced the author "with loving countenance," but his moody reply was, "If a man should pull downe an old stone wall and begyn at the lower part, the upper part thereof might chance to fall on his head." "Venymous wrytynge," Sir Thomas More called it in his reply; but it set light to the train, and the end of the begging friars and the sturdy idle holy thieves was in sight.

The *Ship of Fools* and *Cock Lorells Bote* had some
influence on Coplande's *Hye Way to the Spitel Hous*,
which was published in 1531. He describes how he
took shelter from the rain in the porch of one of those
hospitals that used to take in poor old honest impotent
persons; and how he fell into conversation with the
porter. They talked, naturally, about the inmates
of the hospital, and Coplande told the porter how,
as he walked along toward St. Paul's, beggars lined
the streets mumping together in a most doleful choir.
One mighty stoborne slave whined to Coplande—

> Now mayster, in the way of your good speed
> To us all four behold where it is nede,
> And make this farthyng worth a halfpenny
> For the fyve joyes of our blyssed lady,[1]

and, as a reward for his patron's generosity, offered
to recite Our Lady's Psalter three times. At length
some honest serving man tossed the old palliard a
penny; whereupon he pulled forth eleven pence
more, and, turning to his companion, cried, "Let's
go and dine, make revell and gaudy chere and fill
the Pot!" So long as the shilling lasted he could be a
gentleman; and off lurched these nightingales of
Newgate down the street, "swerynge as they were
wood." The hangman, Coplande remarked at the
end of his conversation, shall lead the dance at the
end . . .

Card-sharpers, cozening butchers, gluttons and
other familiar sailors in the Ships of Fools were
satirized in the *Wyll of the Devyll*, one of many tracts
written about the middle of the sixteenth century to

---

[1] *Hye Way to the Spytel Hous*, 1531, Sig. B2.

expose the growing abuses of roguery in every walk of Elizabethan life. Its keen insight into knavery and the curious mixture of interest, sympathy and contempt is shared by all the later Coneycatching tracts, making one inclined to suspect most of the Elizabethan pamphleteers of having once been tramps themselves. They protest too much, and the very violence of their adjectives is as suspicious as the denunciations of a Puritan.

It was John Awdeley who first made the distinction between the beggar and the Coney-catcher, and realized that, while the Brotherhood of Beggars was growing among the slums of London and spreading from village to village, there was another band of professional cheats appearing in a rather higher order of society. *The Fraternitye of Vacaboundes* is the real source of most of the Coney-catching pamphlets from Harman to Dekker.

But Thomas Harman had wider knowledge and a greater talent. He had, too, unrivalled opportunities for studying the beggars' organization, being himself on the Kent Commission of the Peace. His hobby was collecting the various types of tramp rambling on the Dartford road, and the *Caveat for Common Curseters* describes the peevish pelting and pinking practices of which Awdeley had given only a "glimsing light." He used to chat with the beggars that came to his door "with fair flattering words"; and then return to his study and make notes of what had passed. It must have pleased his sense of irony to know that "harman" was Pedlar's French for the stocks. Many of the tramps he describes he must have known personally. There is John Stradling with the shaking head: a certain Harry—"he drivelleth when he speaketh"; Lawrence with the great leg; and Richard Horwood, "well nigh eighty years old, he will bite a sixpenny nail asunder with his teeth, and a bawdy drunkard to boot."[1]

By 1566 the twin Brotherhoods of Beggars and Coney-catchers had reached their full strength; and the war against them was not to be confined to pamphleteers.

War had been declared against the earliest un-organized rabble of beggars as early as 1351 when the futile Statute of Labourers exasperated the villeins to rebellion. It was followed by an attempt in Richard II's reign to forbid unlicensed roaming from town to town, and the placing of stocks in every village in the country. Hundreds were gaoled and whipped to the shire's end. Henry VII released the beggars from prison, set them in the stocks for a day and a night and packed them home to their respective parishes. More and more frequently these wooden engines of penitence figure in the warfare against the tramps, and it is surprising that, though they still stand with their rusty chains in many of the unspoilt villages of England, they should no longer be put to any practical use. Henry VIII resorted to sterner measures. The proclamation of May 26, 1545, against vagabonds who haunted the "Bancke, and such like naughtie places" and by whom "many simple yong men be polled, and some utterly undone," was only the prelude to a series of stringent laws. Licences to beg were issued, but sturdy beggars

---

[1] *Caveat*, 1566, ed. C. Hindley, 1871, pp. 110, 111.

were to be whipped at the cart's tail and, for a second
offence, to have their ears cut off. Edward VI started
a new campaign with one of the most barbarous
laws on the Statute Book. All former Acts were re-
pealed. Any beggar found aimlessly loitering or
any man who had run away from his master was to
be burned with a great V and fed like a prisoner
on bread and water. Should he repeat his offence,
he was to be branded as a slave and have iron chains
fastened about his neck, legs and arms. But it was
Edward VI who realized the chief breeding ground
of the beggars and he was the first to restrict the
number of taverns and wine vaults. Two hundred
more were suppressed in 1575.

Because during her reign the beggars were at
the height of their power, the famous statutes of
Queen Elizabeth were more numerous and more
complete than any of their predecessors. The Queen
herself had actually been mobbed by hordes of
beggars who were camping in the brick kilns on the
road to Islington. They hooted at her, to her great
indignation. But she had her revenge. Houses of
Correction, the Beggars' Borstals, were established;
and there was an attempt to classify beggars under
such headings as fortune-tellers, bearwards, minstrels,
pedlars, pretending sailors and the like. All such
were to be whipped or conveyed to an almshouse.
William Fleetwood, the Recorder, was indefatigable
and regularly rounded up and hanged batches of
criminals. There was a general arrest of masterless
men in 1569, and more than thirteen thousand
were imprisoned.

But all this seemed to have small effect. The

Watchmen, the "pewter-buttoned, shoulder-clapping Catch-poles," had been gradually becoming more and more inefficient since 1285. Their favourite practice, it was said, was to enter a tavern under pretence of searching for a criminal and thus obtain from the terrified landlord a tankard of free beer. They were always a kind of amateur association, with few talents, in spite of the song of James Gyffon—

> A constable must be honest and just,
>   Have knowledge and good report,
> And able to strain with body and brain
>   Else he is not fitting for't.

Common citizens acted as unpaid policeman, much as they act to-day as jurymen. Until the eighteenth century the decrepit night watchman was the only paid force besides the military. Verges and Dogberry were helpless against the organized cunning of their foes. The Hue and Cry was one of those queer relics of the primitive days when the angry householder would stand shouting after the thief at the door of his hut, and the members of the clan would gather for revenge. It was never officially declared obsolete, but was allowed to die gradually of its own inefficiency and to remain, like the ducking-stool and the stocks, a quaint link with the incomprehensible past. Only a few street-corner youths had time or inclination to run at a moment's notice bellowing after felons. The parishioners called upon by the Watch for help would often enough refuse it. "God restore your loss!" they would say, "I have other business at this time."

Sterner and sterner measures of repression were

taken. Four times every year the Privy Search was conducted. The civil magistrates combined to round up suspects, and at times entire counties were combed out for criminals. These manhunts sometimes resulted in the capture of hundreds of vagrants. In 1569 all the gates of London were watched by specially appointed beadles day and night, so that they might capture the beggars as they swarmed into the city or clambered aboard the Gravesend barges. But in the following year things had grown worse than ever. City Marshals with armed bodyguards were sent to patrol the roads at a salary of six shillings and eightpence a day. At the beginning of the plagues all beggars were banished in a body from the town. Their power reached its height about 1595. They had by then become a menace only less serious than open rebellion, and for years there raged a kind of civil war between the Government and the Brotherhood. In numberless riots the tramps would induce the apprentices to join under their rakehelly standard and sweep the streets. At one time the Mayor saw in martial law the only solution. On more than one occasion there were armed scuffles in the roads and the Provost Marshal would patrol the town with a company of soldiers, round up the stragglers and have them summarily hanged on Tower Hill. Tramp after tramp was "clapt by yᵉ heeles in yᵉ Clinke," and prisons were always full.

The Elizabethan "Compters," the "Rumboe" as they darkly called them, were unlike modern gaols in that they ensured that their inmates would find them a change for the worse. Even the hovels of the Bankside were better than the filth of the State prisons or the brutalities of the Houses of Correction. "In truth," writes a Somerset J.P. to the Lord Treasurer, "work they will not, neither can they, without most extreme pains, by reason that their sinews are so benumbed and stiff through idleness." He points out that they would all rather go to gaol than to a House of Correction. In a hundred years the prisons had not altered for the better, and the foul kennels where Luke Hutton and Geoffrey Mynshul lay "far worse than dogs" could not have been more sordid than the Poultry Compter into which, like swine in a hog's sty, Ned Ward and his friend were flung.

The mixtures of scents that arose from tobacco, dirty sheets, stinking breaths, and uncleanly carcases poisoned our nostrils far worse than a Southwark ditch, a tanner's yard or a tallow-chandler's melting room. The ill-looking vermin, with long rusty beards, were swaddled up in rags, some with their heads covered with thrum-caps, and others with them thrust into the tops of old stockings.

The prisoners were crammed together like coffins in a vault in this subterranean boozing-ken, in that underground cell known as Limbo, where the condemned criminal was chained before his death. Here there stood the great black stone called the Black Dog, on which a candle was set and where it was said more than one desperate felon had dashed out his brains. Geoffrey Mynshul, who had spent miserable days in Newgate for debt, comments on the drunkenness and dirt of prisons—"a place that hath more diseases predominant in it, than the Pest-house in the Plague-time, and it stinks more than the Lord Mayor's Dogge-house or Paris-garden in August." A few dirty benches and a wooden table were ranged against the wall, and the floor was trodden mud. According to other writers the walls glistened with the slime of snails and spiders big as bumble bees spun their webs in the dark corners.

Many were the devices for punishing the unruly tramp. In the middle of Cornhill stood a strong wooden cage, containing a pair of stocks and a pillory. This was expressly designed for "Night-Walkers." The stocks were the most venerable of all instruments of shame, for were they not employed to humiliate the Prophet Jeremiah by the High Gate of Benjamin? The stocks outlasted the pillory, but they were not a more popular method of punishment by ridicule. Very seldom was the massive pillory of Cheapside without its occupant, thus publicly "refuging his shame," and dodging the missiles of a delighted mob. But the pillory seemed as ineffective as the prison, even when it was followed by a whipping at the cart's tail. The two usually went together—

> And then they are taught a fine trick,
> to look through a piece of wood;
> And oftentimes when they are found thus
> with pain they do follow the cart.[1]

Whipping was the commonest punishment of all; and London must have been a distressing city to live in, for "lamenting wretches" moved daily in procession through the streets, bleeding under the Beadle's lash. Harman gives a savage woodcut of a lewd leuterer hanging half-naked to a pole,

[1] *Roxburghe Ballads*, ed. C. Hindley, II, p. 473.

THE SCOURGE AND THE PILLORY

being lashed with birches; and, a hundred years
later, Thomas Ellwood speaks feelingly of the long,
slender twigs of holly which will bend almost like
thongs, and lap round the body. But the Elizabethan
seems to have regarded the spectacle with equanimity,
and the victim of the pillory, the "Stoop-knapper,"
was often, like Defoe, either looked upon as a hero
or completely disregarded. The Law was taking its
course; that was all.

> A common vagrant should by law be stript,
> And by a common Beadle soundly whipt.[1]

The common vagrant was also pierced through
the gristle of the right ear with a hot iron "of a compasse of an inch aboute"; he had a great **S** burnt
on his chest or a yellow **V** sewn on his shirt to remind
him that he was but a slave and a villein; and at
the entry of any strong or sturdie Roag to a House
of Correction he suffered, as a mere formality, "xij
stripes uppon his beare skynne."

The last resort was execution. It was a common
saying that "Tiburne tree must once a month be
topt," and this seemed, after all, the simplest solution
of the problem of vagrancy. "To Tyburne with them!"
cries Stubbes. In hordes they were led up the fatal
hill, while the bellman of St. Sepulchre's recited to
them elevating verses and the priest adjured them to repentance and the ballad-writers scribbled their rhymes.

> Sweet Punck, beere-house, and beere, good-night
>   The honest Roague's departed
> To hanging (by the Justice' spite)
>   To his long home hee's carted.[2]

---

[1] Rowlands, *A Fooles Bolt is soone Shot*, 1614, E3.
[2] Dekker, *O per se O*, 1612, Sig. O3.

Most of them ended their brief days at a rope's end. Harrison notes that not one year passed without three or four hundred swinging from Tyburn's wooden horse. The executioners, Bull Derrick, Dun, Ketch, were kept busy enough. A few of them suffered a more exalted fate; for it is curious to read of a strange engine at Halifax where, by an ancient tradition, thieves were always guillotined. This machine was a square wooden block with an axe-head fastened in it and sliding up and down between two posts. It fell "with such violence that, if the neck of the transgressor were as big as that of a bull, it should be cut in sunder at a stroke, and roll from the body by a huge distance."

If the wretch refused to plead either guilty or not guilty he was pressed into compliance. He was laid in a "lowe, dark house" naked on his back with his legs and arms drawn by ropes to opposite corners of the room. On his chest "irons and stones so much as he may beare (or more)" were placed. "And the nexte daye he shall have three morsels of barley bread withoute drinke." And—"so till he dye. . . ." As much as four hundredweight was put on the chest of the highwayman Phillipps before he pleaded.

It was not till the middle of the seventeenth century that the point of view of the beggars was seen with any sympathy. It was then that a certain Mr. Stanley of the Inns of Court (a reformed highwayman) pointed out that a beggar was whipped or otherwise "hounded according to law" for being idle, however anxious he might be to work. Sir Balthazar Gerbier suggested that professing Christians should be compelled to leave part of their estates to the penniless; and about the same time there was an agitation against the death-penalty as a punishment for the theft of anything over the somewhat arbitrary value of thirteen pence one halfpenny.

But it was many years before it was realized that one of the main causes of beggary is indiscriminate generosity. Hannibal Baskervyle says Antony a Wood "was so greet a cherisher of wandring beggars, that he built for them a larg place like a barne to receive them, and hung up a little bell at his back-dore for them to ring when they wanted anything." Had he lived in the sixteenth century, he would not so often nor so promptly have been "indicted at the Abendon sessions." Like most governments faced with a crisis, the authorities had been inclined to follow the example of Pantagruel, "to enquire further into things and then do what shall be reasonable." They had at first attempted to crush them underfoot by sheer brutality, then to force them to work, irrespective of whether there was any work for them to do; and finally by establishing some means of State support.

Not till the time of Edward VI was the army of the beggars assessed at its true strength. Its degrees were mapped out by Holinshed thus:

I. The poore by impotencie	The fatherlesse poore mans child.
II. The poore by casualtie	The wounded soldier. The decaied house-holder. The visited with greevous disease.

III. The thriftlesse poore   The rioter that con-
                                    sumeth all. The vaga-
                                    bond that will abide
                                    in no place. The idle
                                    person, as the Strumpet
                                    and others.

Almshouses were established, an enormous number
of them in Queen Elizabeth's reign. The poore by
impotencie were housed in Greyfriars' or Christ's
Hospital; the poore by Casualtie in St. Thomas',
Southwark, or St. Bartholomew's in Smithfield; and
the last and most numerous order found grim hospitality within the walls of Bridewell.

But this did not mean the end of the campaign.
James I, the Hammer of the Tramps, cleared all
the pedlars out of London, making it an indictable
offence to set up a booth outside a house. In 1614
a heavy blow was struck by the Lord Mayor, who
dispatched numbers of vagrants to Bridewell, suppressed the stews and restricted the inns. A Surveyor
of Vagrants was appointed to stir the constables
to their duties; and in 1618 divers idle young people
were carted off to Virginia. Finally, in 1690, a Society
for the Reformation of Manners was founded, designed, says Strype, to controul Looseness and to
check those "disempering themselves by an excess
of drink." But by that time the war was won; the
Beggars' Brotherhood was disbanded, and England
was soon to be darkened by the ponderous shadow
of the House of Hanover.

IV

THE BEGGARS

THE two most significant events of the Elizabethan Age were the coming of the beggars and the battle of the Armada: and there is at least as much reason to couple them as to couple Waterloo with the playing-fields of Eton. For half that peerless and incomparable crew which defied the Spaniard was recruited from the Brotherhood of Beggars.

It is curious that it should be just at this time that the Gypsies appeared from nowhere. They were a different race from those that mumped on the highway or nipped the casual bung at St. Paul's Walk.

> Pindy pandy rascal toys,
> We scorn cutting purses;
> Though we live by making noise,
> For cheating none can curse us.[1]

Half the romance that has gathered about them is due to the mystery of their coming. They appear always in literature as they appeared to Tom Jones and the terrified Partridge on that lonely midnight road to Coventry, gay but sinister, the harmless daemons of a Limbo half way to Hell. It was suggested that, when the Turks conquered Egypt, many of the Egyptians fled over to Transylvania and thence scattered, roaming from land to land; but even in those days their Egyptian origin was not generally believed. "Ptolemy, I warrant, never called them

---

[1] Thomas Middleton, *The Spanish Gipsy*.

Bampfylde Moore Carew,

King OF THE Beggars

his subjects," says Dekker, but the mere suggestion
that they hailed from that ancient and mysterious
country was enough to set them apart from the
beggars. Beggars were creatures of the daylight,
sitting in the sun by the church door or limping
down the crowded highways of noon. Gypsies were
born under Mercury and travelled by night; the
minions of the moon went by the moon and the
seven stars of the Pleiad, and were mistrusted alike
by citizen and rogue. Even in those days they were
the picturesque magicians so often described in
fiction; even then they were "wholly addicted and
given to novelties, toys, and new inventions, delighting
. . . with the strangeness of the attire of their heads
and practising palmistry."[1] For their queer powers
of conjuring and prognosticks these wretched, wily,
wandering vagabonds were objects of fascination
and fear, and were proud to claim that they owed
service to none but their mistress the moon—

> The Moon's my constant Mistresse
> & the lowlie owle my morrowe.
> The flaming Drake and the Night-crowe make
> Mee musicke to my sorrowe.

"Beggarly in apparrell, barbarous in condition,
beastly in behaviour,"[2] they had appeared from
somewhere vaguely in the North at the beginning
of the century. Their headquarters were, like those
of the beggars, said to be in Derbyshire. By the
time Meriton Latroon had listed himself one with
the ragged regiment they had become a small but

---

[1] Harman's *Caveat*, vii.
[2] Dekker, *The Belman's Second Night Walke*.

highly organized army, travelling from place to place and living chiefly on other people's poultry. Like the beggars, they had officers and ranks from king to commoner, and like the beggars they spoke their own peculiar jargon. They would send small advance guards to spy out the fatness of the land, and these, like disreputable boy scouts, would mark the route they had taken by chalk-marks on the walls or bundles of sticks significantly arranged, a practice which they taught the Brotherhood of Beggars, and which has survived to the present day.

Their name they borrow from the Moone, because, as the Moone is never in one shape two nights together, but wanders up and downe Heaven, like an Anticke, so these changeable-stuffe-companions never tary one day in a place, but are . . . the onely base Runagates upon earth.[1]

Perhaps because of this alien remoteness, and perhaps also because, though they were feared for their ill-doings, they were admired for their picturesque clothes, their juggling tricks and mysterious knowledge, they have endured centuries longer than the Brotherhood of Beggars, and linger even now "a quiet, pilfering, unprotected race."

The Gypsies, however—the Moon Men—are not my concern. With their swarthy faces, their knowledge of magic, their life of sunlight and of stars, they were objects of mingled wonder and derision to the Elizabethans. They were a band of outlaws of a different race, unlike that secret and sinister society that was slowly growing to power about the walls of London.

The beggars had come. Ragged and lowsy with

---

[1] Dekker, *The Belman's Second Night Walke.*

bag, dish and staff the ryf-raf haunted the highways
in increasing numbers, living with haws and hunting
the blackberry, as Coplande innocently remarks.
Every night they filled the sheep-cotes, the Pounds,
the hay-lofts, and the porch of St. Bartholomew's
Church. Puckridge, Hoxton, Lancaster were already
notorious for them. Not many of the passers-by
knew the dark truth about their lives: and to toss a
Harington to a beggar was an easy penance for sin.
The Elizabethans had grown up with the vagrant
and his clapper: their Hallowmass puling had been
a cradle song.

"Bless your good worship!" So the canting chorus
would begin—

> One small piece of money——
> Among us all poor wretches——
> Blind and lame!
> For His sake that gave all!
> Pitiful Worship!
> One little doit![1]

So the whining chorus, the characteristic beggars'
"chaunt" would ring down the road. Some gallants
gave because it was a gesture that pleased them and
flattered their importance; some through mere weakness, like Sir Thomas Browne who never passed a
beggar by in his life without relieving his Necessities
with his purse or his soul with prayers. It was a
paying enough game: but it had behind it the laws
of a complicated technique. These noonday mumpers
depended entirely upon their revolting personal
appearance and their cunningly insinuating words
to stir the pity of the passer-by. No oaths or threats

---

[1] Beaumont & Fletcher, *Beggar's Bush*, II, i.

discountenanced them, for they had long been accustomed to abuse. They had in fact been through a kind of tramp's training school; for they belonged to a Brotherhood of Beggars.

The first duty of the beggar was, as might be expected, to learn to beg. In this subtle and ancient art he was instructed by various tutors, grown hoary in the practice of their principles.

Springlove. . . . Let me hear how you can *Maund* when you meet with passengers. . . . Suppose some Persons of Worth or Wealth passing by now. Note me. "Good your good Worship, your Charity to the Poor, that will duly and truly pray for you day and night——"
Vincent. Away you idle Rogue, you would be set to work and whipt——
Springlove. ——that is lame and sick; hungry and comfortless——
Vincent. ——if you were wellserved——
Springlove. And ever to bless you and reward you for it——
Hilliard. Prethee hold thy peace (here be doleful notes indeed). . . .[1]

Once having learnt the rudiments of their art, they became experts in one or other of the Orders of Knaves. Their infant tongues

Soon learnt the canting art,
Knew all the prayers and whines to touch the heart.

Along every roadside and in every corner of the realm swarmed disbanded military men, still in the tatters of their uniforms and with the jargon of the camp and monstrous strange oaths hot on

---

[1] R. Brome, *A Joviall Crew.* Works (1873) III, p. 395.

their lips. These were the Rufflers. They had come home to a land where pillage and bloodshed were not only unheroic, but illegal; and they were tempted to prolong the jollity of campaigning by preying indiscriminately on the common citizen, the flatcap, the Blog.

"After warres," remarks Rowlands, "it is commonlie seene that those that went out honest, returne home again like roysters: and as they were brent to the warres bottome, they have ever after all their days an unsavoury smacke thereof." This unsavoury smacke made them a kind of inferior order of the Hectors, Roarers, and Bravoes of a more exalted society. They would swagger along the streets, taking the wall of terrified pedestrians, and twirling unimaginable mustachios. "They seeme gallant sparkes," says the old ballad—"*but I know what I know*." They would boast of their exploits in a hundred battles, but, like Captain Bobadil and the Roarers, while they had assurance enough for their ferocious tales, they showed singular ingenuity in avoiding an open quarrel. The Ruffler

> Never turns again, nor dares oppose
> But mutters coward curses as he goes.

When Falstaff had to march to Coventry, it was a company of Rufflers he picked up from the streets, fifty such toasts and butter, with hearts in their bellies no bigger than a pin's head, and as like as not many of them had never smelt powder. It was a usual enough thing for some Idle Apprentice, tired of the monotony of his job, to take to the roads in the character of an old soldier who had served

his country well and whom she had now left un-
gratefully to starve.

If the Ruffler happened to meet with some kindly,
middle-aged woman, he would cringe, tell a pitiful
story of his maiming in the wars, showing some
counterfeit wound and whimpering for a copper—

> Still doe I cry, good your Worship, good Sir,
>   Bestow one small denire, Sir,
> (And bravely at the bouzing Ken
>   Ile bouze it all in Beere, Sir!)[1]

If he met with a man, he might outface him, demanding money after a truculent recital of his
heroisms or a somewhat sinister list of the immense
number of heroes fallen beneath his sword. In his
stories he would have

> slaine more men by breake of day
> Than could have graves digg'd for them in a weeke.[2]

If he chanced upon a fellow-thief, he would crossbite
him, picking his pocket or openly robbing him.
And if he came on some young noble lord or city
gallant, he would say:

> Brave man of Honour, cast a favourable looke upon the
> wounded estate of a distressed gentleman, that hath borne
> Armes for his Countrey in the hottest broyles of the *Nether-*
> *lands*. . . . Fortune hath onely left me a tongue to bemoane
> my losses, and one eye to be a witnesse of your noble
> bounty.[3]

Such an appeal was not easy to resist. The technique

---

[1] *A Description of Love*, 1629.
[2] Rowlands, *Looke to it :For Ile Stabbe ye*, p. 18. (Works, ed. E. Gosse.)
[3] John Taylor, *Works*, pp. 100, 101. (Fol. 1630.)

of blessing the giver before he gave is as old as beggardom itself.

If he escaped being "buried aloft in the air" on
twined hemp, the Ruffler usually ended by becoming
a highway thief, or (for his was one of the nobler

TITLE-PAGE TO COPLANDE'S PAMPHLET, 1531

orders of the tramp's Dectarchy) an Upright Man.

On the title-page of Coplande's *Hye Way to the
Spytell Hous* there is a woodcut depicting the author
in the middle of his famous conversation with the
Porter on the subject of tramps. A little behind him,
smaller and more insignificant, stands leaning on
his staff with a crafty gleam in his eye a typical
Trewand or Hedge-creeper, the type of beggar
known to his companions as an Upright Man. The
Upright Man was the sturdy vagrant who terrorized

the successive Tudor Parliaments, the Maunderer
on the Pad or wandering rogue who tramped the
roads living on berries and sleeping where he could, in
porches or deserted barns or ash-heaps, like Colonel
Jack. His name indicated his physical rather than
his moral characteristics; for he was one of the
few types of beggars that did not resort to sham
wounds, sores or deformities whereby to earn the
bread of compassion. These losels and mighty lubbers were the ancestors of the modern tramp; the
only one of the whole Brotherhood that you may
still meet (but alas, how changed!) walking down the
summer footpaths.

It is the Upright Man who has cast for so long
the same glamour over vagabondage that sentimental
literature has woven about the Gypsies. Strong,
sunburned, free as the air, he roamed from place to
place, from stocks to pillory—

> Heaven was the roof that canopied his head,
> The Cloudes his Curtaines and the earth his bed,

and he lived without regretting the past or anticipating
the future, unless Tyburn threw its long shadow
across his path. It is a life that has always appealed
to the sentimental literary mind or to those that
have never had the smallest opportunity of living
that life themselves. In all the songs and plays of
the Elizabethans the beggar is a rogue, but he is
nearly always a jolly rogue—

> We have great gaine, with little payne,
>   And lightly spend it too:
> We doe not toyle, nor yet we moyle,
>   As other pore folkes do.

We are winners all three,
And so we will be,
   Wherever that we come, a :
For we know how
To bend and bow
   And what is to be done, a.

It needed the stern realism of Burton to appreciate the other and truer side of the picture—the rogues with bare legs, with feet like hoofs: "their discourse is scurrility, their *summum bonum* a pot of ale." Superstitious idiots they are, too, he adds, nasty, unclean, lowsie, poor, dejected, and humble, living on pulse like a hog or scraps like a dog. The juice of the malt was the liquor of his life, and at bed and board a louse was his only intimate companion.

Of this derelict company the Upright Man was second only to the King. When he associated with the remainder of the Brotherhood (for he usually worked alone) he was the bell-wether of the flock and would rouse the beggars from their barn each morning by trolling some genial stave:

To Pimlico we'll go,
Where merry we shall be,
With ev'ry man a Can in's hand
And a Wench upon his knee.

Thus one would like to picture him in the early dawn before the rest of the rowsie mumpers were astir, the brimming tankard in his hand and some such rollicking tavern catch upon his lips. But if he performed the ceremony at all—for others say it was the privilege of the Patrico, or Counterfeit

E

Priest—his song would more likely be some vile stanza of Pedlar's French—

> This is Bien Bowse this is Bien Bowse,
> Too little is my skew,

or—

> With faces of wallnut
> And bladder and smallgut,
> We're come scraping and singing to rouse ye;
> Rise, shake off your straw,
> And prepare you each maw,
> To kiss, eat, and drink till you're bouzy![1]

And, as a rule, he showed a pretty contempt for his brethren, preferring to travel separately, trudging the roads with his pack, the whole kingdom his walk, and a city his parish, finding, in Dekker's words, "in every man's kitchen his meate dressed," and a penny for him to spend in the purse of every wealthy traveller. From house to house he lurched, much abused with beere; and having collected all the money he could, repaired with it to some habitual meeting-place.

Upright Men with their clubs, called affectionately "Filchmans,"[2] in their hands, and some buxom trollop at their heels, were familiar objects on the roads. Often they would act the part of a Ruffler, as did Tearcat, in *The Roaring Girl*; but the roaming eventually became a perpetual flight from the pitilesse hel-hounds of the jayle. For, though the Upright Man was the one most often chosen for King of the Beggars and as the introducer of the "Wild Rogue"

---

[1] Farmer, *Musa Pedestris*, p. 43.
[2] The word, according to Harman, meant Robber.

to the Brotherhood, yet it was also he who most frequently ended by climbing three trees with a ladder and dancing on the empty air.

Rufflers and Upright Men formed but the vanguard of an army of incorrigible tatterdemalions. Most repellent of all these Stibber Gibber knaves were the Counterfeit Cranks and the Clapperdudgeons or Palliards. The Counterfeit Crank was a beggar who pretended to be a sufferer from the Crank, which we more ponderously call Epilepsy. In an age which gravely considered that the bone of a stag's heart consumed by a barren woman enabled the bystanders to behold the glory of God, or that the heart of a turtle dove in the skin of a wolf would render the wearer incorrigibly chaste, it was not difficult to move the hearts and "peck the purses" of the credulous. Awaiting a favourable moment— at the church door (preferably before the service, when the congregation would be in charitable mood), or in the crowded centre of fair or market—the Counterfeit Crank would cry out, fall into repellent convulsions, and, privily clapping a lump of soap between his teeth, foam marvellously at the mouth. The trick was well known, for at the very beginning of the century the *Liber Vagatorum* records the devices of the "Grantners," who would prick their noses with speargrass, and on whose lips bubbles of soap-froth would rise as big as a man's fist.

The most notorious of English Cranks was one Nicholas Genings. One morning in 1566 he was observed by Thomas Harman, who was then lodging in Whitefriars, naked from the waist upwards, saving he had an old jerkin of leather, patched, and that was loose about him, that all his body lay out bare, a filthy foul cloth he wear on his head, being cut for the purpose, having a narrow place to put out his face with a baver made to truss up his beard, and a string that tied the same down close about his neck, with an old felt hat which he still carried in his hand, to receive the·charity and devotion of the people, for that would he hold out from him, having his face from the eyes downwards, all smeared with blood, as though he had new fallen, and had been tormented with his painful pangs, his jerkin being all bewrayed with dirt and mire, and his hat and hosen also, as though he had wallowed in the mire: surely the sight was monstrous and terrible.[1]

Harman, however, being an amateur detective of beggary, had his suspicions when he observed Gening's singular reluctance to washing his face; and set two boys to keep a watch on him. These discovered that, after his day's work about the Temple, Genings would retire to the fields behind Clement's Inn. There he renewed his stains from a bladder of sheep's blood and daubed fresh mud over his legs and arms. When the rogue was at length captured, thirteen shillings and three pence halfpenny were found on him, and after being forcibly washed he was seen to be a handsome stalwart with a yellow beard and an astonishingly fair skin. He combined the profession of Crank with that of Upright Man. The man must have had a genius for disguise— indeed, to rise to any heights in the vagabond's hierarchy required a considerable talent for amateur theatricals. Genings as an Upright Man and Genings as a Counterfeit Crank appear two completely

[1] *Caveat*, p. 56.

different persons. In Harman's woodcut the tall
dignified gallant is altered to a ponderous deformity,
with something elephantine in the folds of bandages

NICHOLAS GENINGS AS AN UPRIGHT MAN AND A COUNTERFEIT CRANK

about his legs, the stoop of the broad shoulders, the
repulsive and pendulous lip.

He escaped with some ingenuity from the constables
and fled naked over the fields. He was heard of again,
pretending to have been a shipwrecked mariner;
but at the last was recognized, taken to Bridewell,

set in the Cheapside pillory and lashed at the cart's tail from one end of London to the other. "His picture," comments Harman, "remaineth in Bridewell for a monument."

The Crank, however, was less laboriously artistic than the Clapperdudgeon, as the Nip was on a lower plane than the Foist. Clapperdudgeons were usually Welshmen, and with the proverbial subtlety of their kind had turned begging to a mysterious and esoteric art.

Victor Hugo has a description of the "Court of Miracles" of the *Argotiers*, which was the origin of the Mystery Parlours of the Clapperdudgeons, and which he describes as an "immense dressing room" where beggars gathered to prepare their wounds and sores for exhibition on the following day.

Then there was a sort of false soldier, a *narquois* as he was called in the Argotian tongue, who whistled away while he was undoing the bandages of his false wound, and unstiffening his sound and vigorous knee, which had been bound up since the morning in a thousand ligatures. On the other hand, there was a *malingreux* preparing, with celandine and oxblood, his *Jambe de Dieu*, a sore leg, for the morrow. . . . In another place a young *hubin* was taking a lesson in epilepsy from an old *sabouleux*, or hustler, who was teaching him the art of foaming at the mouth by chewing a piece of soap. . . .[1]

The Court of Miracles was not cleared till 1667, long after the English Palliards had been whipped to the plantations. But Whitefriars, the London "Alsatia," at its height, the notorious Turnmill Street or the disreputable suburb of Picthatch,

[1] *Notre Dame*, ch. vi.

could have been little better than the slums in the heart of mediaeval Paris.

The Clapperdudgeon fashioned his artificial sores often with considerable ingenuity.

> Crutches, wooden legs, false bellies,
> Forced eyes and teeth——

nothing came outside their scope. But the counterfeit sore was the device they chiefly relied upon to awake compassion. Meriton Latroon fell in with a master-maker of these "clymes," who would mix the rust of old iron with unslaked lime and soap and spread this over a leather strap which he then bound to the leg. When the strap was removed, most of the skin of the leg came with it; blood was rubbed on the sore flesh, a sight Meriton Latroon could "hardly look upon without dropping down." A simpler and less painful method was by the use of

> An old rag with butter, frankincense,
> Brimstone and resin, blood and cream[1].

or ratsbane, which raised great blisters but often rendered the sores incurable. The position of the sore upon the body was a matter of some delicacy. Rufflers always used one on the back of the hand, so that they could pretend to have been kicked by a horse. This was known as "Footman's Maund." The sore placed above the elbow ("Mason's Maund") was intended to be evidence of a fall from scaffolding: and so forth, innumerably. When the sores had been arranged to his satisfaction, the Clapperdudgeon would lie in the muddiest part of the street, gabbling the Lord's Prayer and whining out:

[1] Beaumont & Fletcher, *Beggars' Bush*, II, i,

Ah, the worship of God looke out with your merciful eyes, one pittiful looke upon sore lame grieved and impotent people sore troubled with the grievous disease and have no rest day nor night by the Canker and Worm that continually eateth the flesh from the bone![1]

But the sore was not the only weapon in the armoury of the Clapperdudgeons. The cause of their art was not unattended by greater sacrifices: and they must have been an incredibly tough-minded crew. One of the *Klenckners* (the German Palliards) cut half a putrefying leg from a corpse that swung in chains from the highway gibbet. He tied his own leg out of sight and attached the corpse's limb beneath it; and lay in the sunlight, a living disintegration, by the door of Schletstett Church. "Give them a kick on their hind parts!" says the author of the *Liber Vagatorum*, not unjustifiably. This is certainly some advance on the more primitive method of strapping one leg out of sight as soon as a traveller was observed—

> If the gentre Folke be coming,
> Then streight it is our fashion,
> One leg to tie
> Close to our Thigh
> To move them to Compassion.[2]

Not long afterwards the ballads described how the legs were made to fester,

> And looke all or'e
> Like a raw sore.[3]

Yet in the time of Seneca beggars had been known

---

[1] Dekker, *O per se O*, Sig. N2.
[2] *Loving Mad Tom*, Fanfrolico Press, p. 42.
[3] *The Cunning Northerne Begger.*

to amputate themselves. A ponderous fifteenth-century divine notes that they frequently blind themselves or deliberately make themselves "crokyd" in order to inspire compassion; Barclay had included a Clapperdudgeon in his *Ship of Fools*, and Coplande complained to the porter about those who came stooping on crutches or hobbling on stilts,

> With bloody clowtes all about theyr legge
> And playsters on theyr skyn.

The disreputable game was evidently well worth the candle. The stories one reads in the militant weeklies about beggars who cringe all day in the streets with a monkey and a dirty cap, and at dusk ride home in one of their Rolls Royces to one of their country houses, are paralleled by the old ballads, like the *Stout Cripple of Cornwall*—

> Nine hundred pound this Cripple had got
> By begging and thieving so good was his lot,
> A thousand pound he would make it he said,
> And then he would give over his trade

—except that the Cripple of Cornwall took his last ride on Tyburn tree, and his descendant, I suppose, continues to use his Rolls Royce.

"The House of Correction," says Thomas Fuller, "is the fittest hospital for those cripples whose legs are lame through their own laziness." Houses of Correction were grim enough; but worse was the fate of Master Simpcox.

King. . . . What, hast thou been long blind and now restored?

Simpcox. Born blind, an't please your grace.

Queen. Tell me, good fellow, camest thou here by chance,
    Or of devotion to this holy shrine?
Simpcox. God knows, of pure devotion; being called
A hundred times and oftener, in my sleep
By good Saint Alban; who said. "Simpcox, come!"[1]

Simpcox was an ingenious knave, but he was exposed by Duke Humphrey, whipped till he leapt the stool and lashed through every market town from St. Albans to Berwick.

The Elizabethans grew accustomed to such tricks, and the appalling spectacle of festering legs and cheeks pitifully disastered disturbed them not at all. The bluff was often called; and sometimes the impotent cripple, crutch in hand, would bound along the back streets, pursued by the infuriated Watch. In a pleasant fantasy, Samuel Rowlands describes the County of Theveningen, ruled over by Don Purloyningo. This chieftain invited all beggars to live with him in sanctuary. The Clapper-dudgeons, hearing the news, danced very nimbly with delight.

There you should have seene one that hath beene lame neare fortie yeares, and gone on his Crowches fifteene to my knowledge, throw away his stilts, and daunce the round Morrice.[2]

Once the Clapperdudgeon had been unfrocked, his old profession became too dangerous for him to practise. A Whip-jack was a favourite part for him to play after his exposure; for one would not readily connect a wandering mariner with a tramp suffering from palsy or the falling sickness. These Whip-jacks were fresh-water mariners whose ships

---

[1] Shakespeare, 2 *Henry VI*, II, i.   [2] *Martin Mark-all*, 1610, p. 35.

had been "drowned in the plain of Salisbury," who had, in fact, never smelt the spray, like the last of their descendants, the old man who met Dorothy Wordsworth on the Glasgow road and "spoke cheerfully in a sweet tone." They wandered up and down the countryside with tales of shipwreck on the Cornish coast, persuading the credulous by brandishing documents garnished with huge seals. In an age when the ability to read or write was still something of a talent, a seal was an impressive talisman; and the forged document set forth, with a great array of noble names, the virtues and misfortunes of the bearer. Other carriers of false papers were the Fraters, with letters patent for the Beggars' Hospitals, and the Jarkeman, who forged licences for travelling. Queen Elizabeth, in a proclamation to the High Sheriff of Yorkshire, takes particular notice of these forgers.

And in this case, she remarks, the passeports should be so discreetly sealed, subscribed and written as they should not easily counterfeit the same; which, as it is reported, some of them can readily do; and do carry about with them certain counterfeit seals of corporate towns and such like, to serve their purposes on that behalf.

Of these impostors Chaucer's Pardoner is the ancestor, with his wallet full of forged documents and the pig's bones he brandished as the relics of a saint. He too had the beggar's characteristic liking for a draught of corny ale; and very reminiscent of the friar who accompanied him on the road to Canterbury was the Elizabethan sham priest, the Patrico, bringer

of bound to the border

the *Rule* and *Recorder*

the mouth of your order

as Preist of the game

and Prelate of the same.[1]

Coplande calls him the Patrying Coue, the Pattering
Cove, the Mumbling Bloke; and his genial business
was the fixing up of impromptu marriages among
doxies and Upright Men. Such ceremonies were
as flippant and as rapidly despatched as the wedding
of Audrey and Touchstone, and they were tradition-
ally performed under a hedge. Parson Underhedge
the Patrico was sometimes affectionately called,
and he adjured the young couple to

live together in the fear of the Lash, to give good example
to the younger Reprobates, to beg within Compasse, to
escape the Laws of the Justice, the Clutch of the Constable,
the Hooks of the Headborough, and the biting blows of
the Beadle.[2]

While the happy pair went through the ceremony
of leaping over a dead horse, the Patrico mumbled
his pedlar's Abracadabra. But to him was often
assigned the less mystical duty of rousing the Brotherhood from their barns by an early morning hymn.
There survives an amusingly scurrilous *Sermon in
Praise of Thieves*, which might have been the Sunday
Morning Address of one of these Patricos. It points
out that most of the great Old Testament characters
were also great robbers, and concludes, with emphatic
conviction, "thus may you see that most of all God
delighteth in theves."

[1] Ben Jonson, *The Gypsies Metamorphosed*, 1640, p. 7.
[2] R. Brome, *A Joviall Crew.*

Among the lesser orders of the Beggars' Brotherhood were the Dummerers, who had acquired the trick of doubling back their tongues so as to make it appear that they had been born dumb. Their favourite story was that they had had their tongues cut out for speaking disrespectfully of the Prophet Mohammed. Dummerers persisted in their tricks for centuries, and in George Parker's day were known under the name of the *Tolliban Rig*. They were said then to tie a thread to the end of their tongues and "communicate" this to some paste which they then swallowed, thus drawing the tongue back and securing it. . . . There were a number of Kinchin Coves. These were small boys kept on a special reducing diet so that they would be thin enough to worm through pantry windows.

> We want a boy extremely for this function,
> Kept under for a year, with milk and knot-grass . . .
> Robin the red tinker had a boy . . .
> Would have run through a cat-hole.[1]

And there were the Priggers of Prancers, an attractive euphemism for Horse-thief, whose profession was an art in itself. The advantage of being a Prigger was the speed with which the booty could remove itself together with the thief to a safe distance. These at least will survive in one form or another, till the car becomes as obsolete as the horse.

But more numerous than any other of the orders of vagrants was the creature known as Tom a Bedlam, the Abram Cove.

During the Middle Ages, on certain appointed

[1] Beaumont & Fletcher, *The Coxcomb*, II, ii.

days, the more harmless inmates of the twelfth-century Hospital of St. Mary Bethlehem in Bishopsgate, the "madman's pound" as it was later called, were given leave to go out in the streets and beg. John Aubrey remembered seeing these wandering idiots who had come "to some degree of sobernesse," and notes that they were given a tin badge to wear on their left arms as a form of licence. This Hospital was the earliest of several madhouses, and subsisted largely on charity. But there was small charity in the attitude of the average Elizabethan towards lunacy. Two centuries before, Langland had called the lunatics "God's minstrels"; the Elizabethan called them "anticks," and found them as much a source of amusement as the drolleries of Tarleton. He paid a penny for the privilege of entering the Hospital; and regarded the morbid spectacle with that mixture of admiration, amusement and disgust which children feel in the booth of the Fat Lady. The noise of the place was appalling; the "cryings, screechings, roarings, brawlings, shaking of chains, swearings, frettings, chafings, are so many, so hideous, so great; that they are more able to drive a man that hath his wits rather out of them."[1] But the spectacle exercised a curious, macabre fascination. Lunatics danced before the Duchess of Malfy, making sinister sport on the eve of her death; John Evelyn stept into Bedlam one April afternoon and inspected "several poore miserable creatures in chains," and Ned Ward, after it had been magnificently rebuilt in 1676, wandered in for a morning's entertainment, passing from one caged misery to another and jotted

[1] D. Lupton, *London & the Country Carbonadoed*, 1632.

down his impressions as one might jot down idle thoughts about a visit to the Zoo. The genial contempt and amusement with which idiocy was regarded by the Elizabethans is one of the many barriers between them and ourselves.

But is was a contempt not unmixed with a certain superstitious awe. Madmen were possessed. They were shut up in the dark and loaded with chains, like Malvolio. The Daemon had to be chastised. And Tom a Bedlam had Hoppedaunce in his belly, and the foul fiend, haunting him in the voice of the nightingale, led him through fire and flame, ford and whirlpool, bog and quagmire. He lived at the rim of the real world where spades are spades; he walked where thicket joins twilight, in league with the dark spirits. The charity extended to him was born as much from fear as pity; and one threw him a penny rather as one touched wood at an ill omen or crossed oneself before a corpse.

These harmless and fantastic-spirited creatures roamed the wild heaths of the Middle Ages, begging clothes or money, always eager (like Diccon in *Gammer Gurton's Nedle*) for an odd scrap of bacon. They knew neither home nor kindred; and their strange vagabond life and fantastic speech surrounded them with an atmosphere of poetry and superstition that belongs to the old stories of the Lubber Fiend.

> With a heart of furious fancies
> Whereof I am commander;
> With a burning spear,
> And a horse of air,
> To the wilderness I wander.

With a knight of ghosts and shadows
I summoned am to Tourney;
    Ten leagues beyond
    The wide world's end;
Methinks it is no journey.

There is a woodcut at the head of an old ballad

MAD TOM OF BEDLAM

called *New Mad Tom of Bedlam* which shows this poor vagabond numskull as he appeared to the Elizabethan; half-naked, with berries in his hair, carrying a Sharing-horn and crying:

Poor naked Tom is very dry,
A little drink for Charity.

But it was not long before there appeared men who posed as Bedlamites and wandered about demanding money,

Sometime with lunatic bans, sometime with prayers,

sticking pins and nails in their bare arms, bellowing down the village street "with roaring voices." These "lurkers on the Abram sham" were notable members of the Beggars' Brotherhood, and appearing first in the middle of the sixteenth century, plied for a hundred years their miserable trade.

Awdeley describes them as dressed all in rags, bare-legged and bare-armed, carrying "a packe of wool, or a stycke with baken on it, or such like toy," and speaking of themselves queerly in the third person as "poor Tom." They were familiar figures, with their ox-horn, their cut jerkin with hanging sleeves, their tangled elf-locks, and the ash-stick, with a flitch of bacon on the end of it. The mark of Bedlam they counterfeited easily enough, tattooing themselves with the letters E and R; and for a clever amateur actor the frenzy of the half-wit was not hard to imitate. Uttering hollow hoots, dancing up and down the roads and fetching marvellous gambols, transfixing the terrified villagers with "wilde, distracted ugly looke," they were feared and propitiated wherever they went. "Good Worship," they would mumble as you passed, "Master. . . . Bestow your reward on a poore man that hath lyen in Bedlam without Bishopsgate three years, four moneths, and nine dayes. . . . And bestow one piece of your small silver towards his fees, which he is indebted there. . . ."

F

Or they would lean over the back gate of a cottage and shout in raucous, idiot tones—

Now Dame, well and wisely; what will you give poore Tom now? One pound of your sheepes feathers to make poore Tom a blanket: or one cutting of your Sow side, no bigger than my arme, or one piece of your salte meate to make poore Tom a sharing horne. . . . Ah, God blesse my good Dame (well and wisely) give poore Tom an old sheete to keepe him from the cold, or an old dublet, or jerkin of my Maisters, God save his life![1]

They would seldom mump at the highwayside, but would stride over the heath shouting at the sky on their aimless wanderings. Some of them were merry enough and welcome guests at the village fairs; though they were continually in the stocks or at the cart's tail. Others were dark, deceitful and morose. Such a one was John Stradling with the shaking head, a deep-dissembling knave with a cozening tongue, sinister as blind Pew. He claimed that the shock of his master's death had given him a paralytic stroke. His master had been Lord Charles Stourton, hanged at Salisbury in 1557 on a silken halter for a peculiarly atrocious murder. Stradling was one of thousands. There seems something profoundly degraded in the mentality of men who could earn their precarious living by aping the misery of the mad; and pleasanter fellows were the tinkers and pedlars who, at the outskirts of the Brotherhood of Beggars, thronged the streets and cheated customers with glib tongues and snatches of naughty balladry.

The Pedlars, the "Swygmen" as Awdeley calls

---

[1] Dekker, *O per se O*, Sig. M3.

them, and their fellow-vagrants the Tinkers, had
been attached to the Brotherhood since the days
when Chaucer's pilgrims rode from the Tabard
Inn. Tramping down muddy lanes with his pack
across his shoulder and singing some tavern catch,
the tinker was a sight familiar enough in days before
the remotest country lane became decorated with
the progeny of the Home and Colonial Stores. That
merry tattered crew which Izaak Walton found
arguing behind a hedge had no doubt a pedlar
amongst it; and the song trolled to them by the
youngest Dell—"Frank Davison's song, which he
made fortie years ago"—was just such a chorus as
might have been on the lips of Autolycus when
Frank Davison was alive.

> The world is ours and ours alone;
> For we alone have world at will.
> We purchase not, all is our own;
> Both fields and streets we beggars fill,
> Nor care to get, nor fear to keep,
> Did ever break a beggar's sleep.
> Bright shines the sun; play, beggars, play!
> Here's scraps enough to serve to-day.

Autolycus, with his gay cynicism, his light-hearted
contempt for respectability, is their type; and it is
a type not seldom to be found in Elizabethan drama.
To every fair the pedlars crowded with their trays of
linen and crape and

> Gloves as sweet as damask roses,
> Masks for faces and for noses,
> Bugle bracelet, necklace amber,
> Perfume for a lady's chamber.[1]

[1] *Winter's Tale*, IV, iv, 220.

The contents of their packs had not altered much since Tudor times or Chaucer's; Heywood's pedlar (no unworthy brother to Autolycus) also specialized in woman's trifles, in

> Gloves, pynnes, combes, glasses unspottyed,
> Pomanders, hookes, and lasses knotted,
> Broches, rynges, and all maner bedes . . .[1]

The pedlar had always been regarded as an Eulenspiegel, an irrepressible, unsentimental jester, genial, gay, obscene, delighting the village wenches with ribald ballatry, and occasionally increasing his income by most methodically canting the maims of a Counterfeit Crank. It was a profession that lent itself to Coney-catching or beggary readily enough, and these "Irish Toyles with their wallets" were frequent riders of the wooden horse and guests of the pillory. "If," says Overbury, "he scape Tyburn and Banbury" (a town as famous for its tinkers as Stamford for its tramps) "he dies a beggar." Their cozening devices and devilish deceits made them a byword.

Tinkers were rascals of the same breed, full of mischief and ready to make holes in your kettles should you not prove free enough with your money. They were notorious as being the greatest fighters and swearers in the kingdom; and it was to this order that the infamous Cock Lorell was rumoured to have belonged. Like the wandering rogue in one of Beaumont and Fletcher's plays, the tinker with his trull lurked in the woods or the ale-house till night gave them a chance of investigating neighbouring hen-roosts.

[1] John Heywood, *The Foure PP*.

'Tis bitter cold. A plague upon these rogues,
How wary they are grown! Not a door open now,
But double barred. . . . Let's shog off
And booze an hour or two; there's ale will make
A cat speak, at the *Harrow*[1]

They haunted the copses and thickets with their
pike-staff, their bloodhound and their drab, some
down-at-heel wench who, because of the bag of
trumpery goods she hawked, became known as a
Bawdybasket. *Lavengro* gives some picture of a tinker's
life in more degenerate days; but Belle was no characteristic Doxy. The Bawdybasket was the chief
of the female vagabonds, who prowled the forest,
accompanied the brethren of the road and ordered
their transitory homes.

There were others. There were the Glimmering
Morts, who pretended that their homes and husbands
had been burnt, and that they were left destitute;
the young Dells, who still preserved their precarious
virginity, and the Doxies, who had long forgotten
the meaning of the word. Harman met with one of
these last, a certain Bess Bottomley, "surely a pleasant
harlot, and not so pleasant as witty," and chatted
with her across the garden gate. She was lonely:
all her men had been hanged some seven years
before, and "they had been good, loving men." She
shrugged her shoulder at Harman's grieved astonish-
ment. "Alas, good gentleman," she said, "everyone
must have a living," and she waved her hand to
him as she went off down the highway to join in
the mustering of the Damn'd Regiment.

[1] *The Coxcomb*, II, ii.

V

THE BROTHERHOOD

THE best of Greene's Coney-catching pamphlets, that brilliant dialogue between Laurence and Nan (two rogues lying in bed and arguing cheerfully about their sins), ends with this sentence:

Thou hast told mee such wonderous villanies, as I thought never could have been in women, I meane of your profession, why you are Crocodiles when you weepe, Basilisks when you smile, Serpents when you devise, and the divels cheefest broakers to bring the world to destruction. And so Nan lets sit downe to our meate and be merry.[1]

It might serve as a motto for the whole fraternity of vagabonds—sin, eat and be merry. Indeed, these were the three chief elements in the lives of these immoral wayfarers. During Greene's lifetime the Brotherhood had grown to twice the size it had been in the days when Cock Lorell set forth on his village Odyssey. Rufflers, Clapperdudgeons, tinkers, tramps, invested travelling with the same excitement that was given to it in later days by the masked and booted highwaymen of the ballads. A new population, homeless and tradeless, a rowsy rabblement of rakehells, was let loose on society. Their life became inevitably the life of the tramp or the thief; the end for which they lived what Harman calls "Boozing and Bellycheer."

I have described some of the causes that led during

---

[1] *Disputation, Betweene a Hee Conny-catcher, & a Shee Conny-catcher*, 1592. Bodley Head Qtos.

the sixteenth century to the formation of this company
of Maunders. By 1600 they had become a nation,
the Catterpillers of the Commonwealth, as they
are so continually called. It is clear that in the latter
half of the sixteenth century the power of the beggars
was a serious menace to the whole community.
The citizen was helpless and terrified; the government was savagely exasperated and, as a rule, futile.
In the north of England the roving bands were more
feared than the mediaeval marauders. What made
them formidable was not merely their desperation
and the fact that they had nothing to lose, but that
they were for the most part composed of discharged
soldiers. They had a rude discipline of their own,
and at the end of a campaign hundreds of these
moneyless soldiers would be set down at Plymouth
to wander aimlessly across the country or to band
together in a descent on the big towns. In 1589 five
hundred of these beggars became out of hand and
threatened to sack St. Bartholomew Fair. There
was a panic; the soldiery was ordered to disperse
the mob; the town was put under martial law.
For months the presence of the Brotherhood paralysed
London.

It was the appalling number of them that seemed
to fascinate and terrify the Elizabethans. Strype
put their numbers at 23,000 in 1569; and by the
end of the century there were 12,000 in London
alone. "It is not yet full threescore yeares," says
Harrison, "since this trade began"—and yet he
estimates their strength at "above ten thousand,"
and suggests martial law as the only effective method
of dealing with them. This apparently meant little

short of massacre. "This enormity," adds Greene, "is not onely in London, but now generally dispersed through all england, in every shire, city and town of any receipt." And Dekker speaks of them over and over as a hostile army; even suggesting that the plagues were the just punishment for the outrages they had committed.

> Hark, hark, the dogges doe bark,
> The Beggars are coming to Town!

The old song might have served well enough as the Marseillaise of the Brotherhood. Gradually, like an army of the damned, they closed in agrim advance upon the towns. Numbers alone made them a potential rebellion, a focus of discontent: Diabolonians in the city of Mansoul. They terrorized everyone. Edward Hext noted that in 1596 "there assembled sixty in a company, and took a whole cart load of cheese from one driving it to a fair, and disposed it among them." They even threatened justice itself.

A tall man, a sturdy and ancient traveller, was committed by a justice, and brought to the sessions, and had judgment to be whipped, he, present at the bar, in the face and hearing of the whole bench, swore a great oath, that if he were whipped, it should be the dearest whipping to some that ever was. It strake such fear in him that committed him, as he prayed he might be deferred until the assizes; where he was delivered without any whipping or other harm and the justice glad he had so pacified his wrath.[1]

A hundred and fifty years later, the life of a pirate on the high seas or of a rider on the roads, became

[1] Strype, *Annals*. IV, pp. 407, 411.

the Eldorado of the idle apprentices of the towns.
In the sixteenth century to high-spirited Jack Wiltons
and Lazarillos the life of the beggar was as romantic
as that of the soldier in the Netherlands or the sailor
over the world's edge. Although most of the darker
crimes have been committed under the merry greenwood tree, that life still appeared jovial, exciting
and pleasantly brief. In the eyes of the adventurous
there was even something heroic about the beggar.
When the sun was up he roamed the streets, every
man's enemy. Both food and lodging he wrested from
the respectable—

> Each city, each town, and every village
> Affords us either an alms or pillage.
> And if the weather be cold or raw,
> Then in a barn we tumble in straw;
> If warm and fair, by yea-cock and nay-cock,
> The fields will afford us a hedge or a hay-cock;
> *A hay-cock, a hay-cock, a hay-cock, a hay-cock,*
> *The fields will afford us a hedge or a hay-cock.*[1]

Nor was it so easy to condemn and despise the beggars
themselves, if they were men of the stamp of Gamaliel
Ratsey. There was a certain inevitable sympathy
with these ill-doers, as there had been with Reynard
the Fox. Reynard may have been a knave, but he
was certainly no fool; and knavery may be shocking,
but it is never tedious.

> Well fare the wit that makes the world a gull,

—the world being the world of pomposity, stupidity
and imperturbable respectability. For it is only
easy to condemn those sins which we can imagine

[1] R. Brome, *Works*, 1873, III, p. 365.

ourselves committing: for anything which we are
quite incapable of doing, even if we wished, we often
have a secret admiration. "The World, my Dear,
hath not such a contempt for Roguery as you imagine."
The beggar (that ideal, non-existent beggar so
attractive to youth) was a merry cynic, preying on
the mass-stupidity of mankind. Even the mumper,
who spent his life acting a sham, never deceived
himself; and there is an appealing lack of sentimentality about many of their old songs—

> A Craven my Father, a Maunder my mother,
> A Filer my Sister, a Filcher my Brother,
> A Canter my Uncle, that car'd not for Pelf,
> A Lifter my Aunt, and a Beggar myself.[1]

So, among the unemployed who were compelled
to beg and the unemployables who could do nothing
else, were a number of wanton youths and Tyburn
sprigs, who took to the highway with a beggar's
staff and dish in much the same spirit as that with
which they might start out to-day armed with a
pedometer and a haversack. "Avast, to the pad
let us bing!" And if the road ended at the foot of
Tyburn Hill there would have been brave doings
by the way.

In more than in the general similarity of their
morals the Brotherhood of Beggars anticipates the
even more depraved and desperate brotherhood of
pirates in the eighteenth century. Pirates also had
their elaborate codes of behaviour, their stern discipline and their ceremonial boozings. They had
their elected captain, the most daring of the crew,
and beneath him in due gradation the quarter-

[1] Farmer, *Musa Pedestris*, p. 26.

master and the junior ranks. Like the beggars they
too divided their plunder according to the status
of each member of the crew. Their beginnings were
the same and their ends—except that the beggar
swung in tar and chains at Tyburn, and the pirate
lay washed by the tides of Wapping Old Stairs.

In every part of England the procedure of the
Beggars' Brotherhood seems to have been more or
less the same. Like all true gangs they had their
initiation ceremony. Dekker has described how,
wandering one day in a green and secret grove
by a stream whose "noyse went like a chime of bels,
charming the eyes to sleepe," he came upon a little
hut. He entered and found himself in the thieves'
kitchen, empty except for one old nimble-tongued
beldame. She was persuaded to hide him in a loft
from which he watched the entrance of the tramps.
This was one of their meeting-places, where they
would gather to share their spoils or plot the next
move against their enemy the Law. There was a
novice to be enrolled that day among the company.
The chief Upright Man took a "Gage of Booze" in
a great tankard. After assuring himself that the
neophyte was a true rogue, he poured the contents
of the tankard over the kneeling man's head, gravely
pronouncing the words—

I doe stall thee to be Rogue, by vertue of this soveraigne
English liquor, so that henceforth it shall be lawful for
thee to *Cant* (that is to say) to be a *Vagabond* and *Beg*. . . ."[1]

The newly-elected Rogue, the Crank Cuffin, then
recited a long oath of obedience to the rules of the
Order:

[1] *Belman of London* (Temple Classics).

> I, Crank Cuffin, swear to be
> True to this fraternity,
> That I will in all obey
> Rule and order of this lay. . . .[1]

Every beggar was given a nickname on his entry to the Brotherhood, names that were crudely descriptive of their appearance or physical powers: Hye Shreve, Great Bull, Madam Wapapace. He was presented also with the Ten Commandments, drawn up long ago by some ignominious Moses—

I. Thou shalt keep faith with thy fellows.

II. Thou shalt keep the counsel of the brothers.

III. Thou shalt share in all matters of the brotherhood.

IV. Thou shalt not hear the brotherhood ill-spoken of without seeking vengeance.

V. Thou shalt see thy fellows want nothing to which thou canst help them.

VI. Thou shalt share all winnings.

VII. Thou shalt keep true appointments or meetings by day or night at any place so decided.

VIII. Thou shalt not divulge the secret of the canting tongue.

IX. Thou shalt harm no fellow-maunder.

X. Thou shalt take Clothes, Hennes, Geese, Pigs, Bacon, and such like for thy winnings.

The Upright Man who performed the ceremony was the elected King of the Beggars, the Rector Chory or Dimber-Damber. He was chosen by general vote and acclaimed by shouts, clappings and the waving of disreputable bandanas.

> Thou art chosen, venerable Clause,
> Our King and sovereign, monarch of the *maunders*,
> Thus we throw up our *nab-cheats*, first for joy,
> And then our *filches*; last we clap our *fambles*,
> Three subject signs.[2]

[1] *Life of Moore Carew* (T. Price, 1768).
[2] Beaumont & Fletcher, *Beggars' Bush*, II, i.

The custom of electing a king went far back to the days when outlaws in the greenwood chose the most fearless knave among them to be their Robin Hood. It was a similar office to that of King or Queen of the Gypsies; and equally powerful privileges accompanied it. Margaret Finch was perhaps the most famous Queen of the Gypsies. This was the lady who spent so much of her life hugging her knees and puffing at a long pipe that her sinews contracted, and when she was buried at the age of a hundred and nine she had to be put in a gigantic square coffin. She was immortalized on the sign of a boozing-ken called Gypsy House. Moore Carew was one of the more notable beggar kings. The earliest of them were called Master-Wardens, or Clewners, who, as a kind of royal prerogative, dressed up as priests or doctors. There had been great men among them in the older days. One of these, named Solomon, is said to have kept his court at "Foxe Hall" in the time of Henry VIII, and seems to have been a direct forerunner of those Napoleons of the modern underworld who can, with a few machine guns and an amenable lawyer, terrorize a whole nation. Many of them grew fantastically rich. Samuel Horsey, one of the more recent kings, having no legs used to rock himself about the streets of London on a kind of carriage; and by thus exhibiting his infirmity was enabled to buy several large houses.[1] It was their duty and privilege to initiate rogues, to plan details of any proposed assault on the strong-

---

[1] Sam Horsey himself emphatically denied that he was ever king of the beggars. Indeed, by his time, if it existed at all, the title was largely a courtesy one.

holds of Respectability and to appoint places of meeting. "Clause" was their hereditary title, like the Egyptian Pharaoh. Clause was king of the beggars before Moore Carew took his place; and Izaak Walton's tramps referred their dispute to "old Father Clause" when they met with him at the inn named Catch-her-by-the-way, near Waltham Cross.

The meeting-places where the king held his tattered courts were usually in some lonely part of the country, in barns or ruined out-houses. There were beggars' barns at the Three Cranes in the Vintry, at the Draw-the-Pudding near Harrow and the King's Barn at Rotherhithe. The owner of the barn was terrorized into allowing the beggars to occupy it. They billeted men on him like an invading army, and if he made any show of resistance he would find all his ricks ablaze at dawn. Sometimes, as they lay snoring on their heaped rags, some picking knave or nimble prig outside the union would hoist them with their own petard, stealing their day's spoil. That would also result in the burning of the farmer's ricks.

In Meriton Latroon's day they would meet on a little rising grass-plat in Lincoln's Inn Fields, a savage place, holy and enchanted, remote from civilization. The London beggars found sanctuary in the fortress of the Coney-catchers and debtors, Whitefriars, called Alsatia. This suburb was a kind of Beggartown, into which no well-dressed man with a purse would dream of penetrating. The suburbs, the "dark dennes" as Chettle called them, were the worst places in England for beggars; and it is perhaps only by the operation of a natural law of reaction that they should have become to-day the homes of convention and respectability. "How happie were cities if they had no suburbs!" remarks an Elizabethan; and his comment to-day would be equally true with a very different implication. The mumpers of Lincoln's Inn were proverbial; and among these streets a swarm of shadowy distorted creatures prowled, horrible as slugs after rain.

The Tippling House, whether in the town or the country, was their favourite meeting ground. These beggars' "Stauling Kens" stood in the fields and desolate thickets about London, where there was as little chance of being disturbed by zealous watchmen as there is in the stauling kens of more modern rogues—the flats and bungalows in the sorry fastnesses of the suburbs. There they would get rid of their spoils—the beggar, says Edward Hext, "hath his receiver at hand in every alehouse." The moneys would change hands; the tankards would pass round; they would drink themselves upsey-Dutch with mellow beere. There they could "bowl and booze one to another," for the beggar was as often to be found under the ale-bush as under the hawthorn; and Harman considers these disreputable inns among the main causes for their increase. It was here, or on some desolate heath, that they met to arrange the division of the spoil. The mythical "Durrest Fair," where you could see more rogues than were ever whipped at the cart's tail through London, was, according to Dekker, a vast receiving-place for stolen goods, chiefly clothes nipped from houses. The beggars chose a Lord of the Fair to command their tattered troops, and carried various badges or signs to distinguish individual branches of the Brotherhood. Similar marks were chalked up outside stauling kens where stolen property was accepted. Rowlands speaks of a spacious underground cave "halfe a mile in compasse," like a catacomb, where was held a triennial convocation of the beggars of the north. This was probably the Peak Cavern at Castleton; and here they would devise their plans, gather their forces, dye themselves scarlet with ale and make enormous speeches in Pedlar's French.

This queer dialect was Thieves' Cant. Nothing so binds men together as a common secret and a common enemy. The constable was the common enemy and this language the secret that cemented the Brotherhood of Beggars. It was a tongue "composed of *omnium gatherum*," scraps of Welsh, Irish, English, Dutch, Latin. The wandering monks after the dissolution of the monasteries spread such words as *patrico*, a priest, *pannam*, bread; *bung*, a purse, may have been a Cornish word, and there were also a large number of coined fantastic phrases with no recognizable derivation. *Chete*, a thing, was a commonly used suffix, like the Romany *engro*. It created such charmingly simple and descriptive phrases as *crashing chetes*, teeth; *grunting chetes*, pigs; and *lullaby chetes*, children.

The language was said to have been invented somewhere about 1530 and its originator to have been hanged. Dekker has an elaborate story about the tower of Babel. But evidently it was never the conscious creation of one man or one group of men. It must have grown gradually of itself out of the slang of a previous age. There is slang enough in Langland and Skelton; and a few pedlar's phrases are used by Coplande at the beginning of the century. It is clear that the framework of the language existed long before the sixteenth century and the vocabulary increased only because of the rapid increase of its users.

Some of the words were very old. *Crank* and *Dell* and *Booze* had all come from Holland in the Middle Ages. But there is no evidence of the existence of cant before 1500; and within a hundred years it had become largely absorbed into current speech. One or two words, like Togs (from *Togeman*, a cloak), have survived in modern slang. One or two, like "foist" (which originally meant to cheat by concealing dice in the palm of the hand), have acquired the seal of respectability. Underground and invisible like the penny novelette, the language goes unconquerably on, changing beyond recognition with each generation. Dekker points out that there is a kind of Musicke in it; and there are indeed vivid and enchanting words. What could be more delightful than the adverb *benshiply*, meaning "excellently"? A cupboard made benshiply would be a cupboard stout and perdurable, yet whose grace concealed its strength. Colourless beside it is the mere bleak adverb "well." Or there was the forceful and vivid ejaculation *Bing a wast*! for "Clear out!" "Buzz off!"; and for "to sleep" the earthy and genial phrase to *couch a hogshead*—for the tramp seldom slept empty of ale. There is vividness in such words as *Stampers*, shoes; *Heartsease*, a guinea; *Tib o' the Buttery*, a goose—the phrase creates instantaneously a complete picture

G

in the mind. Certainly there was a colour and strength about this beggar language, which Standard English has largely lost; and even if one comprehends only a tenth of the meaning, there still remains a flavour in their songs:

> Frisk the cly, and fork the rag,
>   Draw the fogles plummy,
> Speak to the rattles, bag the swag,
>   And finely hunt the dummy![1]

Thus would they sing at those Neronian banquets held four times a year. Over these unholy revels, like a queen witch, presided a bent and wrinkled beldame, the most ancient bawdybasket of the troupe. The scene is vivid enough—these Clapper-dudgeons and Kinchin Coves, each with his Doxy, bleared and swollen-eyed: Counterfeit Cranks with soap on their lips and hideous scabs on legs and arms: Palliards tearing off false beards with the abandon of schoolboys on a holiday: and in the background some blowsy trull, pink-armed, stirring with a wooden spoon a steam of foaming pottage. It is the revel of warriors tired by the long toil of the day. Each with his bawdybasket, heavy with ale, some shouting, some singing in a din of canting gibberish, the actors in that obscene and noisome drama pass before me. Some one beats suddenly upon a drum, and a cracked voice creaks out the melody of some vile tinker's stave. Round and round the room they dance, grotesque and misshapen, in flapping rags, like monsters in a hideous nightmare. And thus, in a burst of revelry and discord, shuffling round a barn

---

[1] *Musa Pedestris*, p. 82.

dim with smoke and haunted by old smells, this alien
and unspeakable crew fades slowly out of sight—

> Pedlars, Sluts and Tinkers Trulls,
> Hectors, Bully-rocks and Gulls,
> Whores, Bawds and Pimps, and all the Tribe
> Of Cheats and Cutpurses. . . .[1]

[1] R. Dixon, *Canidia, or The Witches*, 1683, I, ii, 7.

VI

NOTABLE BEGGARS

In the mass they fade from sight, becoming historical legends, half fact, half fiction. As their lives were ignored, so their deaths went unrecorded. There were no comets seen. But here and there a figure rises head and shoulders above the crowd, heroic in his very villainy. Such a one was Jack Rhodes; but he, we are told, repented and became a magistrate. There was Ned Browne, too—tremendous figure! We can see him from this distance but dimly, like the shadow in an astrologer's crystal; and his deeds are too similar to those of Master Skoggan or the pranks of Howleglas to be accepted on trust. In appearance he was a Gentlemanlike companion attyred very brave, and would make out in his cozenings (the old trick of the Ruffler) that he was a "Marshall Man" fallen on evil days. But he improved his story by wearing a wig and a false beard astonishingly dyed; so that, in a single day, a beardless Browne could dine with the gull whom the bearded Browne had robbed. He was no mere Ruffler but a cut-purse as well, knowing how smoothly and neatly to foist a pocket or nyppe a bung. He would walk up and down Paul's with other Damme Blades, looking for likely prey, telling his interminable stories of hardship and heroism in the Low Countries. He was "most apt at swearing and rapping out fearsome Gogs Nownes," and had less regard for convention even than his fellow Rufflers. He ex-

changed his wife with a friend for five pounds;
and when at last he decided to reform and turn
over a new leaf in France, he broke his resolution
the day he arrived, robbing a number of churches.
His friends warned him, and made dark allusions
to the gallows; but he light-heartedly retorted that
the gallows was his destiny—

As I have ever lived lewdly, so I meane to end my life as
resolutely, and not by a cowardly confession to attempt
the hope of a pardon.[1]

Nine times he was forced to flee to the Low Countries,
"to see what Rhenish tasted like," he told his friends;
but, brought to bay at last, he was hanged at the
window of a Dutch house. Standing on the sill, he
told the crowd the whole dark history of his life,
and then merrily jumped off the ledge to nowhere.

There was a fine spirit of defiance in most of these
rogues. Even a Brotherhood of Beggars could produce
men not unworthy of the age in which they lived.
Ballads and broadsides about the deaths of the more
notorious of them were hawked in hundreds round
the streets. There were rhymes about famous murderers like Mrs. Brewen, who was burnt alive in
1592 for poysoning her husband with a messe of
sugarsopps, and famous beggars like the incredible
philanthropist of Bednall Green. After they were
dead the "Repentances" of the criminals were
sold for a penny apiece, as were the humiliating
confessions of the three pirates of Wapping. The
custom still prevails; except that, to-day, instead
of the Confession of the criminal, we have the reminis-

[1] R. Greene, *Black Bookes Messenger*, Bodley Head Qtos., p. 1.

cences of his mother or his maiden aunt. In the
Elizabethan age all these death-bed moralizings
were invented by casual journalists. They were
conventional funeral trappings, like the frivolous
and irrelevant swags of foliage on an eighteenth
century hearse. For the whole idea of a public execution is that it should act as a grim deterrent; and
the victim's "last confession and repentance" was
merely to point the moral.

For the most part the beggars died defiant. "Tush!"
they would cry, "what better is he that dies in his
bed than he that ends his life at Tyburne, all owe
God a death"; and—

Hell! What talke you of hell to me? I know if I once
come there I shal have the company of better men then
myselfe.[1]

They echoed the desperate words of Mr. Wiseman's
companion who, in a great Huff, shouted, "What
would the Devil do for company, if it was not for
such as I?"

Their deaths were often more memorable and
more characteristic of them than their lives. One
writer boasts that "in no place shall you see male-
factors goe more constantly, more assuredly, and
with lesse lamentation to their death than in England."
As they had scorned conventionality during life,
so they scorned it at the end of life, treating the
gallows as a grim jest; and sometimes even cheating
the hangman. "To make dispute with Doctor Stories'
Cap" was a cant phrase for being hanged; and
the dispute was not always ended on the side of

[1] *Repentance of Robert Greene*, p. 11. (Bodley Head Qtos.)

Doctor Story. About 1597 there lived a Devonshire banker named Philip Collins who had sworn that he would never live to swing. A series of atrocious highway robberies had given him the name of the Devil of the West. Six times he was captured: six times he escaped. "Many a good budget and purse did he take" in London, Somerset, Berkshire, and most of the rest of England, till the whole country was in hue and cry at his heels. When finally he was chained in Newgate,

> He gryn'de at the gallows,
> and moad at the moone,
> And sayd he would spitt in the hangman's spoone.[1]

He refused to plead and was pressed to death in the gaol.

I suppose the publicity of their deaths gave some temptation to the exhibitionists. The fear of death was forgotten in the excitement, and the criminal egoist's love of the limelight. Some of them greeted the gallows with curious nonchalance, like Mary Blandy, who asked not to be hung too high "for the sake of decency," or the aggrieved rogue who thought the rope had been too tightly adjusted round his neck and said furiously to the hangman, "Would'st thou throttle me, villain?" Others behaved as if they were popular heroes. When one of the Overbury murderers, John Franklin, was told he had to hang he seemed in no great chafe, but laughed "and daunced carantoes up and down his chamber . . . and tould them that to-morrow they should see how gallantly he would hang." When the hangman

---

[1] *Shirburn Ballads*, ed. A. Clark, p. 131.

attempted to put the noose about his neck, Franklin made a jest and tried to lasso his executioner. "Mr. Doctor" thereupon "used a very grave speech" and adjured him to make some prayer or public confession. "I have come hither to dye," retorted Franklin, "and this is no place nor tyme to make exclamation; I dye justly and am willing to dye, and have long desired this hower."[1]

There was also the notorious "Half-Hanged Smith," who, after being turned off at Tyburn in the usual way, was cut down and restored to life a quarter of an hour later. And there was a creature named Mahoney who was borne off in a coffin after his hanging at the head of a weeping procession. Half way to the cemetery he came to his senses and was so overjoyed to discover himself still alive that he uttered three prolonged and hearty cheers. There seems to have been on the part of most of them a carefree, casual acceptance of violent death as the inevitable curtain to a reckless life.

> Take courage, dear Comrades! and be not afraid,
> Nor slip this occasion to follow your trade;
> My conscience is clear, and my spirits are calm,
> And thus I go off without prayer-book or psalm;
> Then follow the practice of clever Tom Clinch,
> Who hung like a hero, and never would flinch.[2]

Luke Hutton, who was in the habit of celebrating his birthdays by robbing the same number of men as he had years to his age, like candles round a cake, swung at York in 1598 singing, according to the ballad,

---

[1] *Egerton Papers*, Camden Soc., pp. 474–476.
[2] Swift's Poems.

> I called for Wine, Beere and Ale . . .
> And when my heart was in woful case,
> I drank to my friends with a smiling face.[1]

The fate of John Bartendale was a singular one. After swinging on the York gallows in 1634 for just under an hour, he was cut down and buried by the high road. Several hours later a traveller happening to ride past the grave saw the earth heaving as though some prodigious subterranean animal were burrowing beneath it. With commendable coolness he dismounted and, tying up his horse, began to dig. Green with mould and wrapped still in the hideous cerements of the tomb, John Bartendale stepped from the grave, thanked his deliverer and asked him for a lift back to York. When they arrived Bartendale stoically presented himself as a candidate for the next assizes. The pardon he deserved was granted.

For the most part they are names or legends; but Gamaliel Ratsey is still a living and recognizable figure. He was among the earliest of the gentlemen thieves, and retains something of the romantic aura that surrounds the name of Robin Hood. Like Luke Hutton, he was a man of culture, and there is an excellent poem attributed to him in which he repents momentarily of his sorry life and the evil companions who had led him astray—

> Deceiving Syrens, Syrens all to mee,
> A shining shaddowe, but a dreame of golde.[2]

In the seclusion of the village of Market Deeping, his father, Richard Ratsey, brought him up as befitted

---

[1] *Luke Hutton's Lamentation. Bagford Ballads*, II, p. 72
[2] *Ratsey's Repentance*, 1605, ed. J. P. Collier.

the son of an honest and respectable citizen. But Gamaliel showed very early in life that his was a roving nature. There was some dark streak of vagrancy in his blood, and he was still only a boy when he set out, like other high-spirited youths, to the Irish wars under the banner of the Earl of Essex.

When he returned he brought back with his soldier's vocabulary all a soldier's love of quarrels and excitement; and his nefarious career was begun. The first step was taken at Spalding in Lincolnshire. He arrived at a tavern in the town, "insinuated himself into the love and league of a servant maid," and became by this somewhat obscure means the honoured guest of the house. He was even granted the privilege of admittance to the parlour, that hall-mark of respectability. It was here that temptation, in the shape of a wealthy farmer, crossed his path. The farmer asked the hostess of the tavern to act as his banker, and keep in some safe hiding-hole a bag containing forty pounds. With Ratsey as her eager and courteous assistant, she locked the money carefully away in a safe; whence Ratsey at once removed it. Carrying the treasure unobtrusively under his arm, he remarked airily that he was thinking of taking a stroll before dinner; but as soon as the door had shut behind him he fled home to Market Deeping and buried the box in the orchard under the moon.

He had hardly closed the door of the inn behind him before the hostess discovered the loss of the gold, an event which "stroke such a quandarie to her stomacke, as if shee had drunke a draught of small beere next her heart in a frostie morning."[1]

---

[1] *Life and Death of Gamaliel Ratsey*, 1605 (ed. J. P. Collier), p. 5.

Ratsey was at once suspected. He must have known he would be. Indeed, his crimes reveal him as brave enough and at times witty; but always something of a dunderhead. He was imprisoned and, knowing that he could not escape from gaol even temporarily without money, he revealed the hiding-place of the treasure to his mother; a frail confidante, for she at once (under pledges of profoundest secrecy) told her daughter all about it. Thus in a brief while the story came to the ears of the Justice before whom Ratsey was to be tried. When he knew that his secret had been betrayed, the intrepid thief escaped from his prison in a shirt and, though he was hotly pursued, managed to evade capture. This was not difficult when pursuit meant a haphazard hue and cry from village to village composed of a handful of ignorant clodpolls whose sympathies more often than not were on the side of the culprit. In most of his crude and clumsy exploits Ratsey behaved like a high-spirited schoolboy. On this occasion he defeated the constables by swimming a "very dangerous great water," which he knew they could not cross. Standing, dripping and triumphant, on the further bank he jeered and flyted at them.

The simplicity and impulsiveness of the bumpkin inspired all his exploits. On the road he met a traveller mounted on a magnificent horse. Ratsey's infectious high spirits enabled him to induce the traveller to join in a somewhat pointless practical joke. He was to pretend—because it was a May morning and the birds were singing in the woods—that he was Ratsey's servant. This was to afford each of them occult and inexhaustible amusement. It also meant that Ratsey rode the traveller's horse. When they came to an inn Ratsey found it an easy matter to persuade his new servant to join him in tankard after tankard, drinking to the success of their up-roarious joke; till at length the unhappy traveller began to fell Oakes in the Taphouse, or (less decora-tively) passed into a tipsy slumber. While he slept Ratsey sold the horse to the landlord of the inn and went off down the road with twenty pounds in his purse. This same mixture of audacity and crudeness brought success to the trick whereby he held up a party of nine men. Ratsey was sitting under a hedge making a tramp's dinner off hazel nuts when he saw the riders approaching. Without hesitation he sprang to his feet and, peering over the hedge, shouted directions to mythical companions, telling them to man the ditch and put half a dozen men at the corner of the road. He then warned his victims that the slightest show of resistance would be enough to draw his entire company upon them; and so robbed them at his leisure.

It was only later that he became a professional and the leader of a gang of thieves. Then he rode about robbing indiscriminately, disguised by a black mask. This he may perhaps have adopted because his hideous appearance made him so easily recogniz-able. His ugliness became proverbial. Not twenty years afterwards Dol Common was thus rebuked by her colleague in knavery:

> I will write thee up Bawd in Paules, cries Face, have all
> thy tricks
> Told in red letters; and a face cut for thee
> Worse than Gamaliel Ratsey's.[1]

[1] Ben Jonson, *The Alchemist*, I, i.

It was only during the last phase of his career that he sank so low. It is pleasanter to remember an earlier episode which reveals his immature sense of humour, and a certain rough clown's kindness he never lost.

Walking one day along the highroad, he fell in with a Cambridge undergraduate. Ratsey began discussing with enthusiasm the subjects his companion had been reading, the *Cosmographie* of Pomponius Mela, perhaps, or the Pandects and Civil Law, till they came at length to a little wayside copse. Ratsey led the way on some pretext; and then turned suddenly on his companion, hurled him to the ground and took his money. Then he cried to the trembling victim, "Rise up, man! Come, I mean not to hurt thee; I would but have thy counsel in a matter." When the undergraduate had something recovered from his alarm, Ratsey gravely remarked that he had much enjoyed his scholarly discourse, and implored him to preach a brief extempore sermon on the subject of Repentance. The scholar climbed on the bough of a neighbouring tree and delivered a fervent address that lasted well over half an hour, Ratsey all the while sitting, earnestly attentive, on a stump. When the orator had at length concluded he was given two of his own gold angels as a reward.

Ratsey grew rapidly bolder, collecting about him a few comrades in roguery, the two chief being Snell and Shorthouse. He passed from one ill deed to worse; yet he never forgot the sermon that the scholar had preached to him in the wayside copse. Years later, having robbed a poor old man, he gave back the stolen purse with an extra forty shillings in it, "for," said he, "the sermon in the wood must teach me to favour and pity them that are poor." Thus, like Robin Hood or Long Meg, he became to his admiring biographer the gallant friend and champion of the oppressed. This he never was. He was merely a travelling knave with a streak of sentimentality in him, wandering from place to place, in search of prey. He was not above crossbiting his fellow-knaves and once sent a picklock to gaol by the simple method of asking him to take a letter to the gaoler, in which he had written a full account of the picklock's deeds.

But in March 1605, he and his companions committed their last crime. He had heard that two gentlemen from Bedford would be travelling home on a certain day, with two hundred pounds upon them. Ratsey waylaid them and made his usual bluff, bullying demand—"I have come for money, gentlemen, and money I must have!" These travellers, however, were made of stouter metal. They at once drew their swords and rode on Ratsey. There was a struggle, during which Snell managed to escape with the money; and the rest of the band fled where they might. Snell hid in London, Ratsey at Saffron Walden. Later they met at a Southwark tavern and shared the spoil. It was Snell who finally brought Ratsey to the gallows. Snell was captured for stealing a horse in Duck Lane. To save his own skin he betrayed Ratsey's hiding-place; and they were both lodged together in Newgate prison. Even then Ratsey's resources were not at an end. By some obscure means he appears to have invented a "water" which could dissolve iron, and had it not been for the chance arrival of a gaoler he might have freed himself from his chains and made a last bid for freedom. As it was he swung in chains at Bedford on the twentieth of March 1605.

Rest go with his rags!

Not less eventful was the career of Long Meg

LONG MEG OF WESTMINSTER

of Westminster. She was a character half-way between fiction and fact, just emerging into reality from the ciphers that caper through the pages of the old jest books. But, although many of the exploits with which she is credited were old stories told and retold through two hundred years, they were stories that centred round a living and vivid personality.

Long Meg was a Lancashire girl who came up to London to seek her fortune in the days of Henry

VIII. She was a "lustie bounsing rampe," according to Gabriel Harvey, a roynish rannell and most dissolute gillian-flurte,

> as long as a crane
> and feet like a plane
> with a pair of heels
> as broad as two wheels———[1]

at all events, a healthy well-built countrywoman. She won a free passage to London by the simple and primitive expedient of beating the carrier till he offered to drive her up for nothing. There was small subtlety in her deeds and she was in no way one of the brotherhood of Coney-catchers; but rather a friend of the beggar and the terror and admiration of the Watch. She settled at Westminster and became barmaid of the Eagle Inn. It was here that she established herself as the first of the Roaring Girls, as the protector of stray vagabonds and the receiver of their stolen spoils. There were innumerable stories of her feats of strength, the duels she fought, the cozening cheats which she exposed or performed. She was an exemplary barmaid, and had a sure way with refractory customers, even with Vicars. One of these Lubbers of the Abbaye tried to crossbite her over his bill, crying, "Oh thou foul scullion, I owe thee but three shillings, and one penny and no more will I pay thee." Meg straightway lent him such a box on the ears as made him reel again; she laid hold of him and beat his bald pate against the wall till he paid up in full. She tapped insolent bailiffs on the head with quart pots: and if any

---

[1] Ben Jonson, *Fortunate Isles*, 1624.

stale Cupturse came in, thinking to pay the shot
with swearing, "Hey! Gogs! Wounds!" she would
have him out of the door in a trice. She stood no
familiarity from tramps; and one of the rules of her
tavern was that if any Ruffler made a brawl he must
pay for it either by standing a bout at quarterstaff
with her or be beaten out of the house by her servants.
"If anyone ask you who banged your bones," she
would cry in her coarse, jolly way, "say Long Meg
of Westminster once met with you!"

She answers to one's idea of the typical barmaid—
a creature so very seldom to be found behind a
bar—and her one aim in life seems to have been
to walk around in search of "means to be merry."
She had a crude sense of the comic, and was "of
quick capacitie, and pleasant disposition, of a liberall
heart, and such a one as would be sodainely angry,
and soone pleased."[1] Her chief amusement was
striding along twilit streets dressed up as a man and
hoping for adventures. This habit was largely the
cause of the interest she aroused among the journalists
of the day—the pamphleteers and ballad-mongers—
as to-day it would be the cause of columns in the
evening papers. These epicene women were admired
in the sixteenth century, and dozens of them appeared
between the days of Long Meg and the drearier
days of Anne Bonny and Mary Read. They used
to fight in the Low Countries; and there are a number
of dubious stories about Long Meg's adventures
at Boulogne, where she served as a laundress. Her
end was in sad contrast to the boisterous story of
her prime, for she is said to have become a brothel-

[1] T. Deloney, *Gentle Crafte*, ii (ed. Mann).

H

keeper, and to have died, repentant and obscure, in melancholy senility at Islington. There is a story that she was buried under a portentous slab in the cloisters of Westminster Abbey, told by what the author of the *Worthies of England* calls with some scorn "a late lying pamphlet." There is also a story that she never existed at all, but was either a milestone or a cannon. . . .

But whether in actual fact she fought her duels in Moorfields and battered the crowns of constables in Whitefriars or was only a coarse popular figure round which these legends grew, she was typical enough of the Brotherhood to which she belonged. All over the country naughty losels like Genings, thieves like Gamaliel Ratsey, jolly evildoers like Long Meg spread with their cheatings; but in London itself was growing to power another brotherhood that neither owed nor admitted allegiance to the King of the Beggars. The members of this league walked not in rags but in satin doublets. They did their mumpings in a more subtle fashion, not at the gutter but in the parlours of the smartest Ordin-aries, or in the thronged courtyard of St. Paul's. They were not beggars imploring alms, but hawks swooping on their ignorant prey. And they called themselves the Coney-catchers.

PART TWO

THE FRATERNITY OF CONEY-CATCHERS

VII

ELIZABETHAN LONDON

THE old maps give one a curious impression of the busy compactness of Elizabethan London. It was "a wooden . . . inartificial congestion of houses," notes a Frenchman of the time, commenting on the haphazard huddle of the buildings. Still it was a thousand times nearer the walled city of the Middle Ages—or of the early Jews—than that amorphous hive of activity it has since become. It is incredibly difficult for a modern Londoner to picture that cluster of spires and pinnacles round the scarred magnificent spire of Paul's: the sails on the Thames: the top-heavy buildings on the Bridge, glittering in the smokeless air. It was a small and splendid city of spires and crowded red roofs, surrounded on three sides by green, lonely woods and fields, and on the fourth by a river poets could still call silver. From the top of St. Paul's or the Tower you could see over the whole circuit of the town; not merely looking upon frozen waves of brick and stone, but on a thousand gardens and green spaces within the city. Yokels drove their herds down the quiet lanes of Marylebone and Chelsea, and could pass from the centre of London to the middle of a field of cowslips in less than ten minutes. On the place where now broods the grim bulk of the British Museum you could hawk or hunt; Islington was a village, "a Solitude almost," says Cowley. And men shot woodcock in Piccadilly and caught fine fish in the brook which gave its name to Conduit Street.

Actually a similar thing was happening then to what, on an immeasurably larger scale, is happening now. The population, which numbered about a hundred thousand, was rapidly increasing, and a cancer of mean ugly houses was already beginning to eat its way mile by mile over the wide fields of Middlesex. In the parish of St. Giles beggars herded together in thousands, living underground in dim foul-smelling cellars. So rapid was the influx of people from the country that dozens crowded together like cattle in the same house, and the streets were thronged with wretches who found no roof to shelter them. From being homeless and unemployed to becoming a member of the Beggars' Brotherhood was no very long step to take.

The river, which was London's chief glory, was also its most important highway. There went the great gilded barges of the Queen and the Mayor under bellying sail; flocks of swans paddled to and fro along the banks; hundreds of private boats and public wherries splashed past the wharfs, and the Thames watermen, following an ancient tradition, shouted abuse at each other over the water. In spite of the dangers of the Bridge, the roar of the mid-tide cataract and the extortion of the watermen, travellers preferred the clean spaces of the river to the noise and squalor of the streets. For hundreds of years the Thames was the main road of London; and, a century after the Great Fire, Doctor Johnson went to Greenwich in a "sculler" from the Temple stairs.

Elizabethan London was full of curious contrasts.

SAINT PAUL'S AND THE RIVER

The splendour of the Temple was within two miles
of the melancholy wastes of Lambeth marshes.
You passed from the glitter and quietude of the
Thames to the narrow, muddy, crowded streets—to
the noise of wheels on cobbles, the creaking of iron
signs, the shouts of the casual hawker. Their cries—
"Hot fine oatcake!" "Whiting, maids, whiting!"
"Have you any old boots?" mingled with "Bonefiers,
belles and peales of ordinance." Dekker vividly
describes the thunder of wheels, the jostling of the
crowds—"hammers beating in one place, tubs
hooping in another, pots clinking in a third, water-
tankards running at tilt in a fourth," the porters
and merchant-men pushing with their burdens through
the crowds and tradesmen passing from shop to shop
intent on their business.

During the day the clamour would swell, and the
mobs of bullies, beggars, sailors, dandies, and apprentices was stilled only by funerals or when the
Whiffler marched to clear the streets for a procession
or when night finally fell. The narrow streets were
lit only by horn boxes containing a tallow dip and
swinging from rare windows. In the gloom the city
became comparatively still; nor, were you a sensible
man, would you venture out after twilight lest one
of the hundreds of lurking thieves or beggars knocked
you on the head for the price of a night's lodging—

That crutch which late compassion moved shall wound
The bleeding head, and fell thee to the ground.

If a mediaeval man came to modern London
he would find the noise familiar; but if a modern
man were to be transported to Elizabethan London,

he would be for some time conscious only of an omnipresent smell, an insidious smell, compounded of the sweat of porters and Smithfield pigs and beggars' clothes. He would find himself in the middle of an unbelievable confusion, a rich fantastic galli-maufry of the grotesque and the beautiful, the sordid and the serene. To discover a windmill next door to St. Paul's was no more incongruous than to pass from the glitter of the goldsmiths' shops in Cheap-side to the foul hovels of the "Bancke," or to find a sermon preached at Paul's Cross, while within the nave of the church the Coney-catchers were counting their stolen spoil. Poverty and knavery stalked at the heels of wealth, as the pickpocket and Coney-catcher stalked their gulls and conies.

Such was the scene in which the Coney-catcher had his deplorable being. The Coney-catcher belonged to a brotherhood of professional thieves; and the "Coney," the "Gull," the "Lamb" on which he preyed was the foolish dandy, the bluff country squire, the wealthy undergraduate or the clod-hopping swain from Devon or the midlands. But the Coney-catcher was a wolf in discreet disguise. The beggar was at once recognizable, for his trade demanded a kind of uniform of wretchedness. The Coney-catcher was disguised as a rich nobleman or a staid and prosperous merchant—or even as a Coney.

Some of them worked by day; others only crept from their evil lodgings at twilight. Diogenes, going his rounds in London, came on one of these Gentle-men of the Cheater's Ordinary and decided that there was "no remedy for such wilde fellowes but to tame them in the dungeon of darkenes."[1] But to many of them darkness was their familiar element. When night fell on the lampless streets the unholy crew gathered for its work. The "dead hour," the witching time when churchyards yawn, was the signal for the coming of the Curbers and the midnight thieves. They waited till the Watch had gone to bed, and then

creepeth forth the wilde rogue and his fellows having two or three other harlots for their turn, with picklocks, hand-saws, long hooks, ladders, &c., to break into houses . . .[2]

But the higher ranks of the Coney-catchers moved easily among honest men, showing their faces openly in the daylight, and trusting more to their fine clothes and cozening tongues than to the secrecy of night.

Not far from Puddle Wharf, near Temple Gardens, was the chief haunt and home of the Coney-catchers, the old Friary of the Carmelites called Whitefriars. This was one of the many "liberties" in the city which had been granted the privilege of being exempt from the royal writ. The mediaeval ideas of sanctuary were rapidly dying, but for another century the rogues of London could find a ready refuge in the precincts of Whitefriars or St. Martin's. After the disbanding of the religious orders Whitefriars was known as "Alsatia," and became a debtor's sanctuary. Actually it was a nest of ill-doers of every kind, from the Ruffler and the tramp to the card-cheat. For over a century it was an autonomous kingdom of rogues whose mere numbers placed them beyond the reach of the law. It was a sanctuary where even the Watch were powerless. "At the cry of 'Rescue!' " says

[1] S. Rowlands, *Diogines Lanthorne*, 1607, p. 12.
[2] W. Bullein, *Dialogue Against the Pestilence*, 1564.

Macaulay, speaking of it as it was in its final stage, "bullies with swords and cudgels and termagant hags with spits and broom-sticks poured forth by hundreds."

It was here that Lord Glenvarloch fled after his quarrel with Dalgarno, but he was forced to disguise himself as a Roarer before he could claim admittance. When he entered he found it a little kingdom of its own, ruled over by a king, "duke Jacob Hildebrod" he was then; "a monstrously fat old man with only one eye,"[1] and with a rigid code of laws. "Alsatia knaves and Newgate dogs" made the place a hell, and for years afterwards the notorious Water Lane was used as a synonym for rogue. Like the thieves' sanctuary of Deadman's Place, it was a crowded slum with every second house a tavern under a creaking sign. Its population was for the most part composed of soldiers from the Low Countries, decayed gallants, Coney-catchers and beggars. Outside the gate by which one entered hung a horn; and one blast on this was a recognized signal that the "old and honourable republic of the Lads of the Huff" was being attacked by the watchmen.

This strange fortress of broken and desperate ruffians was at last suppressed in 1696 by an Act of Parliament.

> The place where knaves their revels kept
>   And bid the laws defiance;
> Where cheats and thieves for safety crept
> Is of her filthy swarm clean swept;
> Her lazy crew that skulked for debt
>   Have lost their chief reliance.[2]

But its place was soon taken. For in 1725 the South-

---

[1] Scott, *Fortunes of Nigel*, ch. xvi.   [2] Ned Ward, *The London Spy*.

wark Mint was freed from the intrusions of bailiffs by charter; and this, transformed to a tramp's sanctuary, lingered on, becoming more and more outrageous till the later days of George the First.

There were other places in London very nearly as bad. There was the Thieves' Sanctuary of Cold Harbour on the Thames, a blind gaunt house it looks in the old prints. Here dubious marriages were patched up without questions, and felons found it a convenient place to hire a boat from their pursuers. And amid the ague-ridden marshes of Southwark stood the ancient and appalling Stews called Holland's Leaguer. This was more a harlot's sanctuary than a home for thieves, but at its height, about 1630, it gave protection to any criminal who sought it. In the old frontispiece to Goodman's pamphlet a halberdier stands by the huge barred door with its portcullis; the moat is spanned by a drawbridge; armed men peer cautiously from the bulwarks. In gardens behind the fort amorous couples sport in summer-houses or on shady lawns. This queer castle of vice, "*bulwarked* on every side, and crosse immured both before and behinde, with deepe ditches, a *Drawbridge*, and sundry *Pallysadoes*,"[1] was supposed to have been built by Dona Britannica Hollandia, the Arch-mistress of Wicked Wenches. As a girl she had been a paragon, a girl who had "a modest cheek rich with bashfulnesse," but conceit led to her downfall. The fair fort of her virtue was constantly assailed, and finally capitulated. There-after, "in unchaste *Progress* . . . from the *Noble* to the *Gentile*, from the *Camp* to the *City*" she became

[1] N. Goodman, *Holland's Leaguer*, 1632, F1.

the most notorious bawd in London. At one time
Moll Cutpurse was intimate with this Venerable
Matron of the Kind Motion; and she was well
known to the authorities. Her famous fortress on
the Bankside was besieged by a force of constables
in 1632, but half of the attackers were drowned
in the moat by the collapse of the carefully doctored
drawbridge. Dona Britannica—worthy prototype of
Mother Cresswell and Moll Quarles—paced the
battlements like a mediaeval baron, giving orders
to her troops:

> We defy
> The force of any man. Who's that knocks so?
> Go, bid the watch look out, and if their number
> Be not too plural, then let them come in!
> But if they chance to be those ruffian soldiers,
> Let fall the portcullis![1]

This Leaguer, where so many gallants had been
despoiled, was eventually starved into submission
and destroyed.

The various brothels or Leaguers were crowded
with Coney-catchers; but the greater number filled
the taverns where money flowed freely and victims
were likely to be found in amenable moods. There
were hundreds of famous taverns in London. Best
known perhaps were the Three Tuns in Newgate,
the Cornhill Mermaid and the Mitre of Cheapside.
Various types of professional men haunted their
several inns—

> Through the Royal Exchange as I walked,
>   where gallants in Sattin did shine:
> At midst of the day they parted away
>   at several places to dine.

[1] Shakerley Marmion, *Hollands Leaguer*, 1632, IV, ii.

> The gentrey went to the King's Head,
>   the Nobles unto the Crown;
> The Knights unto the Golden Fleece
>   and the plowman to the Clown.[1]

Thus the old ballad lists the names of the taverns, getting gradually lower in the social scale till he ends—

> The Swaggerers will dine at the Fencers,
>   but those that have lost their wits,
> With Bedlam Tom let there be their home,
>   and the Drum the Drummers best fits.
> The Cheater will dine at the Checquers,
>   the Pickpocket at a blind ale-house,
> Till taken and tride up Holbourn they ride
>   and make their end at the gallows.

But the haunt of the Coney-catcher was usually a step above the common inn. There were not many inns like the Mermaid or the famous and dignified Devil Tavern of Fleet Street, in whose great Apollo room Ben Jonson ruled his tribe; and there was no place there for the Coney-catcher. His hunting ground was the Ordinary.

The Ordinary belied its name and was a very special kind of restaurant with a gaming room attached.

"That is, in common language, an inn, or a tavern," said Nigel.

"An inn, or a tavern, my most green and simple friend!" exclaimed Lord Dalgarno. "No, no. . . . An Ordinary is a late invented institution, sacred to Bacchus and Comus, where the choicest noble gallants of the time meet with the first and most ethereal wits of the age."[2]

---

[1] *London's Ordinary.* (*Bagford Ballads*, II, p. 106.)
[2] Scott, *Fortunes of Nigel*, ch. xi.

The choicest wits and gallants met also with Coney-catchers, suave, charming men immaculately dressed who would flatter them by talking of the latest doings in Town or the news of the wars on the Continent; and then suggest a game of cards—

> He that will passe into an Ordinarie,
> Let him take heed to deale with cardes and dice;
> Lest whatsoever money in he carry,
> Ere he beware he loose it in a trice,
> And, all too late repentance, learne the price
> To know how he that passeth in purse-full,
> And goes out empty, passeth for a Gull.[1]

These Ordinaries were on a higher level than the taverns, and were perhaps the small beginnings of the Eighteenth Century Clubs. Fashionable men collected there and talked and diced; and it was the ambition of every wealthy or talented youth to be seen daily frequenting the Ordinary. Since the Coney-catcher had himself usually begun as a gentleman or a soldier, he could mix naturally with his peers and fleece them before they knew very much about it. And he moved very quickly from one Ordinary to another, sharing out his spoils either in some lonely field or in the house of a receiver, a "Bell Brow." As the Coney-catcher came from the Ordinary after a good morning's play, meeting another, he would exchange with him some secret pass-word or privy sign. "Quest?" "Twag!" A wink would pass between them, and ten minutes later, in Paul's Walk or Cheapside, they would greet each other as if they had not met for months.

Paul's Walk was the ordinary meeting-place of

---

[1] N. Breton, *Pasquils Passe & Passeth Not*, 1600, p. 2.

the Coney-catchers. This was the central aisle of the church, known also as Duke Humphrey's Walk, the great "waste gallery." Duke Humphrey of Gloucester had been famous for his generosity, but after his death his followers found no one to provide for them. "To dine with Duke Humphrey" was a current jest meaning to go without one's dinner—

> Though little coyne thy purse-lesse pocket lyne,
> Yet with great company thou art ta'en up,
> For often with Duke Humphrey thou dost dyne,
> And often with Sir Thomas Gresham sup.[1]

The jest alluded to those needy loiterers who were unable to beg or steal money enough for food, and wandered in the nave of St. Paul's during that melancholy hour, hoping for charity. It became thus one of the most notorious haunts of broken and desperate men in all London, a promenade for every condition of poverty and wealth; from the tramp and the impecunious nobleman to the prosperous and fur-clad merchant. It was a fashion parade, a money exchange, a centre of crime, gossip and grave deliberations. "O how loathsome a Golgotha is this Pauls!" cries a French visitor. But Dekker regards it more lightly. He advises gallants to show off their strouting Holland slops there; to walk up and down nodding familiarly to any important figure they passed whether they knew him or not. It was there that Bardolph was picked up by Falstaff, and Bobadil proudly boasted of being a "Paul's man."

According to Earle the noise of talking and the

---

[1] I.e. he "walkes out his dinner in Paules, and his supper in the Exchange." Robert Hayman, *Quodlibets*, 1628.

tramp of feet sounded like a hive of bees, a "kinde
of still roare." There hucksters and pedlars cried
their coloured wares; merchants haggled over their
transactions and counted coins into the font; and
wantons kept assignations with their random cullies.
Backwards and forwards through the church passed
wagons of beer and cartloads of stinking fish.

> There squeaks a cart-wheele, here a tumbril rumbles,
> Heere scolds an old Bawd, there a Porter grumbles.
> Heere the tough Car-men combat for the way,
> There two for looks begin a coward fray.[1]

Twelve o'clock was the crowded hour of Paul's,
when the din was at its height. Dekker imagines
the steeple complaining of the Coney-catchers who
lurked in the throng, cheating poor countrymen of
their purses and plotting how they might betray
some wealthy Gull.

> What shuffling, what shouldering, what justling, what
> jeering, what byting of thumbs to beget quarrels, what
> holding uppe of fingers to remember drunken meetings,
> what braving with feathers, what bearding with Mustachios,
> what casting open of cloakes to publish new clothes, what
> muffling in cloaks to hyde broken elbows. . . .[2]

That the nave of their great church should be
the meeting-place of felons and paupers was not the
greatest of the contrasts in Elizabethan London.
Executions had actually taken place in the precincts
of St. Paul's; and it was there that the gunpowder
plotters had been beheaded. Since it was the most
famous and accessible part of the city, here it was
that the latest rumour, the spiciest scandal, the first

---

[1] E. Guilpin, *Skialethia*, 1598. [2] *Dead Tearme*. D4.

news of great happenings were to be found. It was
the obvious place for the encounters of lovers or
the graver appointments of the tradesmen. Every
pillar in the nave had around it its special group.
At one lawyers would discuss their cases, and at
the next a handful of tailors would be reviling the
latest Italianate extravagance in clothes; and at
a third half a dozen merchants would stand mur-
muring portentously about profits. Indeed in this
secular Temple the money-changers did more business
than the priests. They set up here and there informal
booths for the transaction of deals or the payments
of debts. It was on the "fount stone in the Cathedrall
Churche of Saynt paule" that Ralph Radcliffe,
the dramatist-schoolmaster, agreed to pay interest
on his borrowings.[1] But the chink of money
mingled with the hum of casual conversation; for
the nave was also the gathering-place of the
gallants. And where the gallants met, there also
were the Coney-catchers, their obscure attendant
spirits.

In the renaissance of learning, the birth of the
New World and the sudden enlargement and enrich-
ment of leisure, London became more than ever
the centre and focus of the whole land. It was to
remain so for two centuries without a rival. The
fashionable loathing of the country, which is reflected
in so many of the Restoration comedies, died hard.
By tales of wealth, adventure and debauchery,
young men were attracted to the metropolis from
all over the country. A new class came into being.

[1] R. L. Hine, *Hitchin Worthies*, p. 44.

There descended on London a horde of hot-headed, ignorant, spendthrift boys, eager to be in the centre of the strange world where fresh marvels were happening every day. These were the Gallants, the "Gulls," the wealthy sheep whom the wolves of the underworld found easy prey. A "vaine, fantasticke troupe of puffie youthes" swarmed up and down the highways, longing only to see and do all they could in an age when life seemed more than ever precious and precarious. *Carpe diem* was their watchword, as it was the watchword of the gallants of the Restoration; they would all be "damnably mouldy a hundred years hence." But these fantastical magotie-headed lads were not the frivolous cynics of the Court of Charles the Second. They were both unsophisticated and ridiculous, "silly *Huffing* things, three parts *Fop*, and the rest *Hector*"; but they made good soldiers. The Elizabethan age was an age of fustian and bombast as well as an age of fine thinking and heroic action. The great men of the time had great weaknesses. Their follies partook of the magnificence of their virtues. The worme of giddinesse, as John Stephens would say, crept readily into their private purposes. I suppose any period of greatness must throw off a kind of fume or froth of extravagance; and the streets of London were crowded with an astonishing assortment of follies in the age of Shakespeare. Tom Coryat's hastily gobbled *Crudities* could flourish side by side with the enlarged edition of Bacon's grave, sonorous *Essays*. The babblings of a half-wit threaded the dark reveries of *King Lear*. It was not a mere accident of individuality that made men like Essex and Sir

Walter Raleigh half philosophers and high statesmen, and half vain, hot-tempered boys.

The Italianate Englishman had appeared; the young man of means who "completed" his education by travelling to Venice, and returned with a vocabulary spiced with foreign phrases and with his head full of outlandish customs. You could recognize these travelled Gulls by

their gait and strutting, their bending in the hams and shoulders, and looking upon their legs with frisking and singing. . . .[1]

They rode, they ran, they flew to Circe's Court, as Ascham complained; and came home again full of a shallow and frivolous epicureanism.

> Let us drink and be merry, dance, joke and rejoice,
> With claret and sherry, theorbo and voice;
> The changeable world to our joy is unjust,
> All treasure's uncertain, then down with your dust;
> In frolics dispose your pounds, shillings and pence,
> For we shall be nothing a hundred years hence.[2]

A thousand satires and denunciations of their extravagant clothes and habits poured from the Press for many years. Even at the very close of the Elizabethan age Middleton could describe the Italianate dandy as a baboon in man's apparel. His head would be crowned with a tower of white feathers and his face almost hidden by a high, sharp-edged collar that "might have cut his throat by daylight." He would distort himself with the Elizabethan equivalent of plus fours, the balloon-like Holland

[1] James Howell, *Instructions for Forreine Travell.*
[2] Jordan, *Triumphs of London.*

slops, so that his "back part was like a monster's," and his thighs were swallowed up by gigantic boots. Osric in *Hamlet* is a typical example of the Town Gull, the exquisite of the Court, perfumed like a milliner. But there was also the Country Gull, like Master Stephen in *Every Man in His Humour.* The lord of a country manor, down for a market week, was immediately recognizable. He was a grosser cousin of Sir Roger de Coverley; a figure that appears over and over in early drama under such names as Sir Innocent Ninny, George Downright, Sir Ruinous Gentry, and which was a favourite with the writers of the Restoration.

The Country Gull, whether the squire of some Devonshire manor or a cow-eyed, straw-chewing farmer's boy from the North, was a butt to every Cockney, hustled, jostled, fleeced and jeered at by the greenest Coney-catcher. There was also the Gull who wanted to become one of the Swaggering Blades. Hectors and Roaring Boys, the bullies and Bobadils, were surrounded by admiring pupils who would rapturously learn the oaths their heroes used, and paid for their apprenticeship with their purses. These Clotpolls spared no money in the effort to learn to roar like the "brothers of the Blade and Battoune."

Belfond Senior. Well, adad, you are pleasant men, and have the neatest sayings with you; "ready," and "spruce prig," and abundance of the prettiest witty words. But sure that Mr. Cheatly is as fine a gentleman as any wears a head, and as ingenious, ne'er stir, I believe he would run down the best scholar in Oxford, and put 'em in a mouse-hole with his wit. . . .

Sham. O fie, cousin; a company of puts, mere puts!

Belfond. Puts! mere puts! very good, I'll swear . . .

Sham. But Cheatly is a rare fellow; I'll speak a bold word, he shall cut a sham or a banter with the best wit or poet of them all.

Belfond. Good again: "Cut a sham or banter!" I shall remember all these quaint words in time.[1]

In 1569 the first of a series of great lotteries was drawn near the west door of St. Paul's. The lottery of 1608 produced a new type of Gull, the "Twelve-penny Gull," who was duped by Coney-catchers selling forged tickets. Every change produced a new kind of Coney-catcher and a new kind of coney for him to fleece

Dekker wrote a famous satirical pamphlet, the *Gul's Hornebook*, advising the young gallant how to make the most of his opportunities. There was room enough for his Gullery in "this wild forest of fools, the World"; and he instructs them with kindly sarcasm how to arrange the day so as to attract the maximum amount of attention from the gaping "mobile." In Paul's Walk they could spend their legs in winter a whole afternoon; "converse, plot, laugh, and talke anythinge," and in the evening "they might amuse themselves by annoying the police —cozening a whole covey of abhominable catch-polls." An intelligent young man need never be bored. In Paul's too he could hold converse with his tailor, in conspiracy for the next "device"; there he should take note of the fashions of his fellow-ninnies, to have them copied—

[1] Shadwell, *The Squire of Alsatia*, I. i.

> You in the capring cloake, a Mimick Ape,
> That onely strives to seeme an other's shape.

Thus Marston addresses the Paul's Gull. There
he could show off his taffeta-lined gown, call familiarly
to great men, and win his only chance of immortality
by carving his name on the Tower leads.

At the tavern and the playhouse the one object
of the Gull was to keep himself before the notice
of the company, that they might whisper to each
other as he swaggered by, "There goes Such a Gallant!" He was to burst into the theatre very late,
and with much swearing and bustling, push himself
to the stage, where he sat smoking and loudly commenting on the shortcomings of the miserable players.
Advice similar to Dekker's is given in *Every Man
Out of His Humour,* where the hectoring blade Carlo
Buffone instructs the wretched Sogliardo. He must
"sit o' the stage and flout"; provided he was wearing
a sufficiently impressive suit of clothes. He must
"pretend alliance with courtiers and great persons,"
and, as speedily as possible, procure a coat of arms.

Like the Ass in the old fable, the Gull who followed
these instructions was fit prey for the penniless Coney-
catcher—

> All in a flaunt, hee ryots and consumes
> In gold, in silver, silke and sweet perfumes,
> His old Sires' ill-got-goods now goes to wracke,
> Farmes, Forrests, Fields, hee beares upon his backe.[1]

It is the old Sire who has one's sympathy. The sons
often enough wasted their entire inheritance on
their clothes and bore their debts on their "gilded

---

[1] *The Beggers Ape,* 1627. B1.r.

backs." They lived for little but flattery, keeping
up appearances, even though behind them was
nothing but debt. So that a "famished Beau" was
a familiar spectacle in the streets—the wretched
gallant who wandered dinnerless round Paul's in
magnificent clothes, or chewed perhaps an un-
obtrusive crust in the shadow of Sidney's tomb.

> I wonder at so proud a backe,
> Whiles th'emptie guts loud rumblen for long lacke,
> The bellie envieth the backs bright glee,
> And murmurs at such inequalitie . . .
> Ye witlesse gallants, I beshrew your hearts,
> That sets such discord twixt agreeing parts.[1]

These impoverished lackwits were no spoil for
the Coney-catcher, but belonged for the most part to
that historic profession themselves; and the more
intelligent of them lay in wait for a rich heiress or a
gullible young lord eager to be shown the world.
It was the empty-headed stripling with money who
fell so easy a prey to the Nips and Rufflers of St.
Paul's, for

> Two sets of people fills the whole world full,
> The witty Beggar and the wealthy Gull.

[1] Joseph Hall, *Virgidemiarum*, III, 7.

VIII

ROBERT GREENE

SUCH were the Gulls, and such the prey of the Coney-catcher.

The beggars and the Coney-catcher belonged to similar brotherhoods and laid side by side their various traps. But neither recognized the other. There was no communication between them nor the shadow of an alliance against their common foes or victims. The beggar earned his living by pretending to be more abjectly miserable even than he was; the Coney-catcher cheated the Gull by pretending to be his equal or superior. The beggar appealed to charity, the Coney-catcher to vanity— or, with no disguise, they made open war; filling their purse by bullying on the high-road or by systematically sorting the cards and loading the dice.

By the nature of things the beggar was doomed to become rarer, and will ultimately, in a well-organized World-State, disappear. He belonged to a more leisurely age, when travellers still went on foot or horseback, and could be pursued with large and pitiable discourse from the roadside. He belonged to the age of wandering and conversation, of the great title-pages and the interminable folios; the age when men could still believe in the red-eyed Catoblepas or the Manticorn, whose voice was a blend of flute and trumpet; and when one could, like the Reverend Doctor Sibbes, write a grave theological commentary on the *Song of Solomon*, naming it "Bowels Opened." As the vigilance of the State increased, as the number of alms-houses grew, as Poor Laws multiplied and doles and pensions cast their niggard beams on the autumn of his days, the beggar receded more and more into the social background. The truculent mumper gave place to the hawker duly licensed to peddle his wares, or to the street musician dolefully chaunting and backed with some shadow of a claim to be earning his living through a second-hand gramophone. The Coney-catcher, on the other hand, was more often than not beyond the reach of the law. He had followed his nefarious calling in one way and another for hundreds of years in cunningly varied disguises. Fourteenth-century preachers had exposed the gangs of cheats who invited conies to drink with them and then, on some excuse, hurried from the tavern, leaving their guests to pay. They had thundered against the crafty jugglers or the "corsours" at the country fairs who cheated the buyers of horses. The Coney-catcher had changed his tricks but little since those days. He still inveigled rich heiresses into marriage with penniless gulls, drawing for himself a gratifying percentage. He still played profitable but dubious games of skill and floated non-existent companies. But he evolved with the increase of speed into the gangster. He acquired armoured cars and bodyguards of subservient toughs, who, by blackmailing, kidnapping and racketeering, found their proper niche in a swifter and more ruthless world.

It was some time before the Elizabethans realized the independence of these twin brotherhoods. Awdeley had devoted one section of his book to a description of three Gentleman Cozeners, but he gives no suggestion that they were three members of a far-reaching organization. The journalists of the time finally became fascinated by the menace of the Coney-catchers as they had become terrified by the beggars in the time of Harman. Nearly every pamphleteer devoted some of his energies to the Coney-catchers; and nearly every one confused with them the tribes of beggars that had been exposed by Harman. Dekker's *Belman of London* is a shameless and spirited plagiarism of Harman, Greene, Rowlands, and *Mihil Mumchance*, but his racy style and delightfully fantastic imagination made him a favourite among the Elizabethans, and have preserved his works when most of his contemporaries have been long forgotten. William Fennor thought the *Belman* "the most wittiest, elegantest and eloquentist *Peece*" composed by the true heire of *Apollo*. He stole, but he stole in a way that made the theft justifiable. Rowlands also borrowed right and left from his predecessors; and dealt in *Martin Mark-all* with outlaws, beggars and cheats— a muddle of fact and fantasy written in an easy, smooth, and undistinguished style. The word Coney-catcher soon settled firmly into the vocabulary and in a few years became a general name for cheat. In a conversation between Conscience, Feedwell, Nemo and Symon Saywell, Antony Nixon uses it to describe corruption of all kinds—the miserliness of attorneys, the abuses of the Courts, the lamentable inefficiency of churchwardens. The Coney-catchers themselves attacked the greater Coney-catchers of the State. Robert Greene met with some random sharper at a tavern, and reproached him with his way of life.

"Tut, sir," replied the Coney-catcher. ". . . I am sure you are not so ignorant, but you know that fewe men can live uprightly, unlesse hee have some prety way more then the world is witnes to, to helpe him withall: Think you some lawyers could be such purchasers, if all their pleas were short, and their proceedinges justice and conscience? . . . Nay, what wil you more, who so hath not some sinister way to helpe himselfe, but foloweth his nose alwaies straight forward, may wel hold up the head for a yeare or two, but ye third he must needs sink, and gather the wind into begers haven."[1]

"Truth it is," they would say, "that this is the Iron Age, wherein iniquitie hath the upper hande, and all conditions and estates of men seeke to live by their wittes, and he is counted the wisest that hath the deepest insight into the getting of gaines."[2]

There was no real attempt to sift the true from the false. The pamphleteers poured sheet after sheet from the Press to satisfy the demand; they borrowed freely from each other and their forerunners, and took small trouble to ensure that their information was correct.

But the greatest of all the writers on Coney-catching was one who had no need to copy: who took his knowledge from life: and who, openly and with a sort of pride, repented in a London attic of sins "abhominable to declare."

Robert Greene, ex-Coney-catcher and the terror of the lawless, was a queer contradiction. And yet not a wholly inexplicable contradiction, if one remem-

[1] Robert Greene, *Notable Discovery of Coosnage*, 1591.
[2] Robert Greene, *Defence of Conny Catching*, 1592.

bers that the final and fundamental element in his character was moral weakness. Like all weak men he took a strange pleasure in torturing himself with his own shortcomings. He admits that he found his own self his chiefest punishment, and exclaims with Roberto, "Heu patior telis vulnera facta meis!"— though there is no doubt that his masochism was partly a journalistic pose, pandering to the popular craze for Repentances.

A man he was, says Cuthbert Burbie, "given over to the lust of his owne heart." He was an idealist at the same time as he was a sensualist. He was a poet at the same time as he was a thief. Philador, Francesco, Roberto—all those shadowy heroes of his books—are portraits of the same man: a dreamy gallant brought to ruin by a courtesan. His whole life was a struggle, something like the struggle that took place over the doomed soul of Doctor Faustus— alternate riches and pride, poverty and despair, sin and repentance.

His curious weakness of will is illustrated by that passage in the *Repentance* where he describes how a preacher at St. Andrew's Church in Norwich almost succeeded in converting him by the terror of Hell-fire and the banquet of the everlasting and insatiable Worm. "Insomuch as, sighing, I said to myselfe, Lord have mercie upon mee, and send me grace to amend and become a new man." And immediately a party of roisterers dragged him off to the nearest tavern, laughing at his melancholy and drowning his repentance in a pot of ale: Kit Marlowe being one of them, and merry, impecunious, drunken Peele, I daresay.

The scholar and poet spent his days with cup-shot companions in the embraces of the quick and subtile wine. He was tempted ceaselessly by the Infidas and Lamillias of the London slums; and he was haunted to the end of his life by the purity and divine patience of a woman who is the heroine of all his books—who is Isabel or Bellaria, Sephestia or Philomela—and who is, some say, a picture of the wife he had deserted, throwing her out one evening in a drunken fury into the twilight of the London streets.

Gabriel Harvey has given us some sort of a picture of back alleys in Elizabethan London; of the struggling hack, yarking up topical pamphlets to pay for a drink; of the successful playright and penner of love-pamphlets who, after becoming one of the most famous literary men of the time, had not enough money to pay for his last lodging. He was Marlowe's friend, and a man whom Shakespeare pitied and respected. He was at the same time a boon companion of the notorious Cutting Ball, who used to stalk about back streets with a cudgel and a spade beard, looking for someone to bully. Greene the poet was also the "Monarch of Crosbiters and the very Emperor of Shifters."[1] He saved himself from gaol by pawning and pimping. He saved himself from the gallows by turning King's evidence. He even shed a few reproachful tears over his old associates, Nashe, Marlowe, and Peele. Yet in those squalid alleys, dirty, ragged and penniless, he wrote idylls like *Pandosto* and *Mamillia* and created women like Margaret and Dorothea.

[1] Harvey, *Foure Letters* & *Certaine Sonnets*, p. 19. (Bodley Head Qtos.)

The same contradiction—that queer mixture of
profligacy in life and a passionate purity in letters—
is illustrated by his rage at having a bawdy pamphlet
called the *Cobbler of Canterbury* attributed to him.
This was an exhaustive collection of stories about
cuckoldry, "tales told in the barge between Billingsgate and Gravesend." It is illustrated too by the
fervent renunciations of his *Vision*. Like all weak men,
he was continually changing from one extreme
to the other, till finally he changed from Coney-
catcher to policeman. He was a cozener turned
traitor—"a spie," he calls himself, "to have an
insight into their knaveries."

In half a dozen pamphlets published during the
last two years of his life Greene lays bare "those
pernicious slights that have ofttimes brought men
to their confusion." This was the one rag of pride
he clung to, that he had done something towards
revealing the horrible coosnage of the Coney-catcher.
When his tearful ghost appeared to John Dickenson
in 1589, it claimed that the labours of Greene's
last years had "Made a large part of amends for
those former vanities." In those Labours he had
dealt with every branch of the art and profession
of Coney-catching and beggary, giving lists of notorious
rogues and glossaries of Pedlar's French, largely
borrowed from earlier writers.

Those last two years were exciting. The Brotherhood of thieves grew alarmed, and Cuthbert Conny-
catcher retaliated with a sardonic and elaborate
Defence, masking a threat. But Greene was undis-
mayed. He boldly attacked the chief of the band,
one Laurence Pickering, a "notable foist," who

thereafter threw a brick at him from a house-top. He wrote a *Dialogue Between Laurence and Nan,* the subject of which was whether a Foist or a Trull did the greater harm in the world. Nan swore to dig him in the ribs with a Hamborough knife. An attempt was made to assassinate him in a tavern, and he only escaped after a severe struggle. With a kind of frightened obstinacy Greene made a further attack. He promised Chettle he would write a "Blacke Booke," a directory of the names and addresses of all the "nips, foists, lifts, and priggers in and about London." *The Black Bookes Messenger* prepared the way. It appeared in August. All London awaited breathlessly the publication of the promised work. But the Coney-catchers had the last word.

Greene died in September.

He died in something of the emotional panic in which he had lived, and in surroundings of appalling squalor. His only visitor was the sister of Cutting Ball, who had been hanged at Tyburn; the only friend that cared for him was Mistress Isam, and he was at last the prey of unscrupulous scavengers. Dickenson's woodcut shows a bearded, harassed-looking man in a shroud; a cross between a beggar and a monk. "Pitifully blasted and how woefully faded," he sits at a bare table, writing with a quill and brooding mournfully over a hasped book. This was probably Parsons' *Christian Exercise,* which he read as he lay dying, and whose saturnine pages filled his cell with the fiends and flames of an uncomfortably close Inferno. In an ecstasy of terror he wrote his *Repentance,* crediting himself, as men do on their death-beds, with all kinds of exaggerated ill-doings. There is the sincerity of a frightened man in that pathetic recantation. But there is the sincerity of true pride and true penitence in the last two actions of his life. He asked that when he lay dead a wreath of bays should be placed upon his brow.[1]

ROBERT GREENE

And he wrote his last letter to his wife—

Doll, I charge thee by the love of our youth, & by my soules rest, that thou wilte see this man paide: for if hee, and his wife had not succoured me, I had died in the streets.[2]

Which might be taken as a somewhat grim moral for Bohemianism.

[1] Gabriel Harvey, with the clumsy ill-breeding of a pedant, sneered at the poetry and pathos of that act.

[2] *Foure Letters*, p. 22. A more elaborate version of the letter is given in the *Repentance*, p. 32.

Even after he was dead he was allowed no rest. Harvey ruthlessly attacked him; he ridiculed and denounced him with so lunatic a savagery that opinion veered round in Greene's favour. His *Letter* from the other world to Pierce Penniless mentions those who inveighed against his works, his poverty, his life and death, and "omitted nothing that might seeme malitious."[1]

The legend went that he was turned away from Heaven for his sins: and when he tried to find refuge in Hell, he was attacked and driven forth by infuriated Coney-catchers, who naturally constituted the larger part of its population. To this day, it is said, he wanders homeless in a grey and nebulous Limbo of his own, spying out the knaveries of the Brotherhood, but powerless at last to expose them.

[1] Chettle, *Kind Heartes Dreame.*

K

IX

THE NIP AND THE FOIST

AFTER the revelations of the *Black Booke's Messenger* and the other "merrie and pithie Pamphlets," the Coney-catchers invented new shifts and groped their gulls as before. But Greene had struck the first powerful blow against them; and it is chiefly from him that we learn of their organization and methods.

"There are degrees of *Superiority* and *Inferiority* in our Societie, as there are in the prowdest *Companie*"; so the Coney-catcher claimed. But the orders of the Coney-catchers were neither so numerous nor so well defined as those of the Beggars' Brotherhood. We find no meticulous grading from King to Kinchin Cove; there are merely numberless titles, each signifying proficiency in a different branch. They were a kind of Guild of Thieves, and their trade was recognized as a mystery and an art. The names they gave themselves were, like diplomas or degrees, symbols of efficiency in their job.

Two of the most important members of the gang were the Foist and the Nip, or Nipper. These were both pickpockets or purse-snatchers, and belonged to one of the more enduring branches of roguery. The Foist, however, was a step above the Nip. He was usually a "Courtesy Man," and referred to himself always as a "Gentleman Foist." The Nip merely cut the purse and let the coins fall silently into his hand. The Foist held his victim in charming and scholarly conversation while he removed the

TAVERN FROLLICK

entire purse. He was, or had been, a gallant himself; Armin notes that all the best beggars seem to be gallants nowadaies, and Overdo, the J.P. in *Bartholomew Fair*, was so deceived by the cultured appearance of the Foist Edgeworth that he thought him a hot-headed youth led astray by bad company. The gifts of the Foist were thus not merely a cultured appearance and a ready tongue. It was no easy thing to become a successful cozener—"to do that well craves a kind of wit." The three properties of an exquisite Foist, according to Greene, are "an eagle's eye, a lady's hand, and a lion's heart." Shakespeare demands a good nose also, "to smell out work for the other senses." He had to "passe the proudest Jugler alive." His constant study was the Figging Law, the Law of the diver with two fingers. He had to have by heart all the intricate rules of his trade, since his was one of the highest positions in the Brotherhood. The Foist was (and is) an amateur conjuror of considerable skill, for a single slip would be enough to set Old Story's Cap on his head. A mere handshake was sufficient for his purpose. When Ronco, the "cunningest nimmer of Cut-purse Hall," met his old friend Trincalo, he subjected him in his delight to a fervent and prolonged embrace. After which, of course, Trincalo missed his purse.

> He'e gone——
> I'th'devil's name, how could the fellow do it?
> I felt his hands fast locked about my neck;
> And still he spoke. It could not be his mouth:
> For that was full of "dear Antonio."
> My life! He stole't with his feet . . .[1]

[1] J. Tomkis, *Albumazar*, 1614, III, vii.

The expert Foist must spend day after day strolling idly about St. Paul's, Westminster, or the Exchange; and learn how to distinguish at a glance the man who dressed soberly because he liked to, from the man who dressed soberly because he had to.

The gathering-place for Nips and Foists was Duke Humphrey's Walk in Paul's. This was, as I have said, the paradise of the Coney-catcher, like that fountain in Cordova where the innkeeper who knighted Don Quixote practised the dexteritie of his handes. There those smiling, sinister men would stroll easily about, always glancing right and left, either for a victim or a constable. The former were very much more numerous; but, once observed, the chosen victim had to have his attention distracted from the "Bung" he carried at his waist.

This was done sometimes by plucking him by the arm and claiming acquaintance, by accidentally knocking him against a pillar, by pretending to fall in a swoon at his feet, so that he might bend down till his purse dangled invitingly before the swooner's face, or by cruder and more violent methods, such as flinging bags of flour. The trick Autolycus plays on the Clown in the *Winter's Tale* was a characteristic device; and for its execution the Foist had at least to look "courtier capa pe" and have the air of the court in his enfoldings. More elaborate yet was the trick of Latricino, the chief of a band of Coney-catchers in Middleton's *Widow*. He set up as an optician, and found it a simple matter, while he anointed the eyes of his patients with his right hand, to pick their pockets with his left.

But Fairs were their favourite hunting-grounds,

for it was there that the silly country folk who had never heard of Coney-catchers nor read the *Black Booke's Messenger* flocked in their credulous hundreds. In the pleasant old verse dialogue of *The Cheaters Cheated*, a typical scene at a Fair is described. Two Foists, Nim and Filcher, meet with a gaping West-countryman named Wat.

Fil. Stay! prethe who comes here?
Nim. A gaping country Clown.
Fil. Look, how the slave doth stare!
    He's newly come to town.
    He gazeth in the air as if
    The sky were full of rockets:
    Let's fleece him.
Nim. But how shall we get
    His hands out of his pockets?
Fil. Let me alone for that; I lately bought a glass
    Wherein all several colours may
    Be seen that ever was,
    If held up thus with both hands.
Nim. A pretty new design:
    This trick will fetch his fingers out.
Fil. And hey then, in go mine.
Wat. Our Taunton den is a dungeon,
    And yvaith cham glad cham here,
    This vamous zitty of Lungeon
    Is worth all Zomerzetshere . . .

His attention is at once attracted by the coloured glass, which is pressed on him by the two Foists.

Fil. Here, take this glass into thy hand,
    And hold it to thy eyes;
    Thou there wilt see more colours than
    A dyar can devise.
Wat. I cannot zee a colour yet.
Nim. Thou dost not hold it high.

Wat. Che hav't, che ha't, ch'av got it now!
Nim. I faith, and so have I——

and he cunningly lifts the purse; only to find in it nothing but bread and cheese and a few rusty nails.

A common device of these "Fyle-clyers" at the big fairs was to put themselves in the pillory, round which crowds eagerly gathered. While the Nip underwent voluntary martyrdom at the hands of an excited and uproarious mob, his fellow was busy taking unheeded purses. If the trick failed to come off, the Foist only had to drop the purse and swear boldly that he had never touched it, in order to escape scot-free; for at the period no one could be arrested for theft unless he were discovered with the spoil actually upon him.

The Foist and his attendant Nip became so adroit that it would be a clever man who could tell the instant his purse had gone. For the Nip had graduated in a stern school. A certain Master Wotton kept a Cut-purse College in an alehouse at Smart's Quay near Billingsgate, where young Nippers were taught the elements of their art. When, in 1585, the city was raked for felons and receivers, Smart's Quay was destroyed. On the walls they found queer mottoes of the order—

Si spie sporte, si mon spie, tunc steale.
Si spie, si non spie, Foyste, nyppe, lyfte, shave & spare not.

In the seventeenth century it was succeeded by the Academy of Lewkener's Lane where the infant Nip, known then as a "Knuckle," practised on dummies, and the experienced hand "laid plans for his future depredations in the arms of his unsophisticated charmer." Every famous Foist, like every great painter, gathered a school of disciples and imitators about him to whom he taught his methods. Those youthful Nips who showed particular intelligence and skill were known as "Academy Buz-Nappers." One of their tests was the pick-pocketing of a lay figure hung about with bells. It was like the image described by Victor Hugo as a "sort of scarecrow, clothed in red, and so completely covered with little bells and hollow, jingling brasses that there were enow to have harnessed thirty Castilian mules." Charley Bates and the Dodger had not more nimble fingers.

The Figging Law demanded that the Foist and the Nip should work in concert, "pewfellows together and of one religion"; the Foist distracting the victim's attention from the purse which the Nip was cutting. But the Foist had a deep contempt for his clumsier and less adventurous colleague, and, with the spirit of the true artist, disdained even to carry a knife for cutting his bread, lest the dark rumour should go around that he was a mere Nip. He spoke of his companion as a Little Nipper, a term which, even in these democratic days, carries with it a certain air of condenscension. Nevertheless it was the Nip who had the more dangerous task; for he must carry with him the incriminating tools of his trade. He was a "Knight of the knife, a child of the horn-thumb," and the discovery of a cuttle-bung, the sharp blade which slit the purses, or of the curious horn thimble which prevented him being injured by his own tool was sufficient to send a Nip to the gallows. The thimble had to be used with caution; if it were seen the cry of "Horner!" would bring an infuriated mob on the heels of the detected Coney-catcher.

Together the Nip and the Foist haunted the Bank-side, St. George's Fields, where Falstaff and Shallow revelled at the Windmill, and the narrow dark streets among the Bear-gardens. After the theatres were closed these Bear-gardens became notorious for their pickpockets. But the theatres were the ideal places for ambitious Nips. Every John and his Joan, every knave and his quean, says Gosson, crowded together in the Pit, intent on the play, "heaving and shoving, itching and shouldering," heeding nothing else but their companions or the figures on the stage. Among them, a lean furtive shape, glided the Coney-catcher slitting his purses un-perceived. If the cut-purse were discovered in the crowd, the play would be held up and the wretched man hauled on to the stage and tied to one of its supporting pillars in an improvised pillory.

Another favourite place for the activities of the cut-purse or the Foist was under the clock of St. Dunstan's Church in Fleet Street. This was a famous marvel, for on each side of its gilded dial stood two wooden savages who struck the quarters with their clubs. Crowds of long-legged Loobies were always to be found there, gaping skywards, oblivious of the purses at their belts. And up and down the Strand no man was safe—

Here dives the skulking thief, with practis'd slight,
And unfelt fingers make thy pocket light.

They had their specially arranged hours of meeting; and there were various favourite ceremonies which they attended, certain of a good haul—church services, chiefly, where the somnolent or the devout would both prove easy prey. The many triumphal Progresses which Queen Elizabeth made through the streets of London, her visit to Blackfriars in 1600 or the Feast of the Order of the Garter which was celebrated annually on April the 23rd, were for Coney-catchers the equivalents of Derby Day. Amid the press of excited crowds they had unlimited opportunities for the practice of their art. Though there was little fear of detection, they were liable when discovered on such occasions to a summary lynching.

Some pickpockets were great artists in their line, though few names have been handed down to us. Jack Ellis, "the grete pykpurs," as Henry Machyn calls him, was known as the most brilliant of them; and before he was hanged in 1552 had been in every prison in London, including the Tower. There was a certain Mr. Walker who stole, with sublime audacity, a gold watch belonging to Lady Fairfax. He disguised himself as a Commander in the Army and rode forth at the head of a company of fellow Coney-catchers, all dressed as soldiers. One of them secretly extracted the wheel pin of Lady Fairfax's carriage, and she was thus compelled to go the remainder of the way to church on foot. Walker presented himself with a flourish, and, as an officer and a gentleman, gave her his arm. Having a pair of scissors in his hand, it was not difficult for an expert Foist to cut through the chain of her watch while engaging her in genial and scholarly small-talk.

Walker was eventually swung into the next world by the hangman Gregory.

Against such artists as these no defence was sure. Some careful citizens regularly lined their pockets with fish-hooks whenever they went to any public meeting. Their idea was to hook the Foist in the act, like a gudgeon. But the expert retaliated by cutting away the pocket, and sometimes the entire coat-tail, a feat that required no small skill. The endless war was waged remorselessly on each side.

One cutpurse often preyed on another; there was no honour among Nips. A creature known as a Cloyer or Snap dogged new members of the company of cut-purses, "and snaps will have half in any booty." They haunted the inexperienced Nips and Foists, sticking to them "like Burres." Theirs was the tech-nique of double-crossing, or crossbiting, and unless given their "snappage," a tenth share of the spoil, they would denounce the Foist to the crowd. It was a profitable system of blackmail. The notorious Jack Rhodes once served out one of these Cloyers in his own coin by dressing up as a nobleman's servant and accusing the unhappy blackmailer of being a thief, as soon as he had seen him pocket his snappage. The terrified Cloyer handed over all the money he had, and Rhodes shared the spoil with a fellow Foist. A pretie pranke of Wilie-beguily.

Women Foists were scarcely less adroit than men. Indeed Nan makes out a pretty case for their superi-ority:

Yes, Lawrence, and (we are) your good mistresses in that mystery, for we without suspition can passe in your walkes under the couler of simplicitie to Westminster, with a paper in one hand, as if we were distressed women, that had some supplication to put up to the judges . . . when God wot, we shuffle in for a bung as well as the best of you all.[1]

Their end was Bridewell, the grim building in New Bridge Street which had once been a royal palace. The Governor of it used to sit with a little wooden hammer in his hand, and the culprits were lashed till he knocked on the table. The walls resounded with cries of, "Oh, good Sir Robert, knock! Pray, good Sir Robert, knock!" Nan's shoulders trembled at the name. But if a woman Foist were taken in the act she was often summarily executed by the mob. In any case punishment was swift and ignominious. They were sometimes hanged in great batches like sheep. "The sam day was hanged at Tyburne xvii: on was an old voman of lx yere, the strongest cut-purs voman that has ben herd off." Such is a characteristic entry in the Diary of Henry Machyn.

But they were a cheerful, impudent crowd, and showed a healthy lack of conscience or remorse for their misdoings. "Sirrah, if thou dost not mend thy manners, thou wilt shortly be hanged," cried an angry Justice of the Peace, "or I'll be hanged for thee!" "I thank your Worship for that kind offer," replied the Foist, unperturbed, "and beseech your Worship not to be out of the way when I shall have occasion to use you."[2] They did not care who their victims might be. William Kempe, one of the most popular clowns of the age, during his famous dance was followed out of London by two Nips, but the "Dy-doppers" were discovered, blooded

[1] R. Greene, *Disputation*, p. 14. (Bodley Head Qtos.)
[2] John Taylor, *Works*, 1630, p. 182.

at the Whipping Cross and sent back to Town; a more merciful fate than that meted out at Newark to a "nimming gallant" who had been cutting all the purses of King James's court. James had him summarily and quite illegally hanged.[1] No place was free from them. "A cut-purse," says Nicholas Breton, "will be at his work when the thief is at the gallowes." It was a flourishing trade; the wicked men prospered in their business "with a certain kind of smiling felicitie"—that ingratiating geniality which was the chief talent of the Foist.

There were elaborate degrees and offices among the cut-purses. There were Grand Nips and Little Nips. There were various Wardens and Stewards; and a Treasurer to whom the day's takings were handed over at prearranged meeting-places. To such an assignation Edgeworth and Nightingale used to repair after the day's toil. "All the purses and purchase I give you to-day by conveyance," whispers the Foist, "bring hither to Ursula's presently. Here we will meet at night in her lodge and share."[2]

But there was also continual jealousy between the various branches. There was a long-standing feud between the city Nip and his colleague of the country. Country Nips used to travel from one fair to another; and St. Bartholomew's, held for a fort-night every year at Smithfield, was their favourite haunt. Here, like obscene birds of prey, the Knockems and Edgeworths would flock, hungry for the purses of sleepy rustics like Cokes. On these occasions

---

[1] *Narrative of the Progress and Entertainment of the King's Most Excellent Majesty*, T.M, 1603.

[2] Ben Jonson, *Bartholomew Fair* II, i.

notable cozenings were achieved by the Foist who
worked in concert with some trusty Nip. Edgeworth
and Nightingale in Jonson's play were partners
of this kind. Nightingale would attract a crowd
by singing some lamentable ditty, noting as he sang
those men who looked promising victims, spying
out the fattest purses. Then he would tip the wink
and Edgeworth nipped the purse, privily handing
it over to the ballad-singer. This was the most
dangerous part of the proceedings. With pleasant
irony Nightingale sang a stave against cut-purses—

> But O, you vile nation of cutpurses all.
> Relent and repent, and amend and be sound,
> And know that you ought not, by honest men's fall,
> Advance your own fortunes, to die above ground;
> > And though you go gay,
> > In silks as you may,
> It is not the highway to Heaven (as they say).
> Repent then, repent you, for better, for worse,
> And kiss not the gallows for cutting a purse.
> Youth, youth, thou hadst better been starved by thy
> > nurse,
> Than live to be hanged for cutting a purse.[1]

At the conclusion of the song he hands over a copy
of the ballad to Edgeworth, who, as he receives it,
slips the stolen purses into Nightingale's hand.

As numerous and still less popular were the Knights
of the Post. These members of the Coney-catcher's
Brotherhood were very useful to the Foist, for they
were professional false witnesses who, for some trifling
consideration, cheerfully committed perjury. They
were, says Dekker, "daily selling their soules for a
few shillings." They would smug themselves up in

[1] *Bartholomew Fair*, III, i.

borrowed clothes, wearing great seal rings on their hands, and appeared before the judge as moneyed and respectable citizens, who could vouch for the innocence of the accused and put up a substantial bail. A bag of gold and a pint of old sack stopped the mouths of these "Lords of Lob's Pound." They were always roaming about in idle groups, ready to be called upon by distressed criminals; but they were known to the law, and not left unnoticed by the pamphleteers. Chettle recounts with glee that he had seen one of these abnominable false-witness-bearers promoted to the pillory. The only talent they needed was an impressive exterior.

In his attire he is neat and fine, and in his speech stately, with a long piccadevant after the French cut, and of a scornefull countenance, and when he comes into West-minster Hall, he bends his browes, as if he would beare downe the Kinges Benchbarre with his lookes.[1]

Nips, Foists and Knights of the Post were to be found among any collection of people, seeking their dark occasions. But their chief home was amid the squalid fastnesses of Whitefriars and Moorditch, which, being undrained, was to Falstaff a most unsavoury simile. Out of the shadows of those noisome streets would come creeping forth that sinister and ill-scented company, staves under their arms and adjustable beards ready for emergency. And then, from some street corner, would rise a sudden shout of "Clubs!" and the local Dogberry would clatter to the fray. Usually the victim was fleeced, the Foist escaped to hunt down another quarry—

---

[1] *Discoverie of the Knights of the Poste*, 1597, Civ.

> Ten miles unto a Market
> I run to meet a miser,
>   Then in a throng
>   I nip his Bung,
> And the Party ne'er the wiser.[1]

Roaming thus about the twilit streets were incalculable numbers of such stray Coney-catchers. Fennor compares them to Owles that hide by day, and to dogges of Aegypt that skulk from their dens, dodging here and there, till they reach the haven of a Tavern. Some of them were experts in more than one branch of the art of Coney-catching, and could

> play the *Foist*, the *Nip*, the *Stale*, the *Stand*,
> The *Snap*, the *Curb*, the *Crosbite*, *Warpe* and *Lifte*,
> *Decoy*, *prig*, *Cheat*,

living in scorn of Tyburn and the rope's ding-dong.[2] They had begun their life by learning the art of picking pockets or by snatching a random apple from a stall, and had gradually worked their way up till they could qualify for the gallows—

> Some *thieves* are like a *Horne-booke*, and begin
> The ABC of filching with a pin;
> Their Primmer is a point, and then their Psalter
> May picke a pocket, and come neare a Halter,
> Then with long practice in these rudiments,
> To break a house may be his accidence. . . .
> Untill at last, to weare (it be his hap)
> A Tyburne Tippet, or old *Stories* Cap.[3]

With the energy and ambition of the proudest merchant they must devote their lives to the perfect

---

[1] *The Blind Beggar.* (*Wit and Drollery*, 1682.)
[2] John Taylor, *Brood of Comorants*, fol. 1630, p. 8.
[3] John Taylor, *Comparison betweene a Thiefe and a Booke*, p. 115.

mastery of their trade; for a false step could never be recalled, and the gallows waited always for them. They had learnt their dark wisdom from their fathers, and practised it all their lives.

> Every one duly knows his Part,
> They have conn'd their Lessons all by heart.
> The curious faculty of Hooking,
> The ingenious Art of Gentile Rooking . . .[1]

Chief among those Coney-catchers who obeyed no particular "Law" was the Courtesy Man. Antony Nixon describes one whose

cheekes were plumpe, and red, as a cram'd pullet, and covered with red rose leaves, his lookes chearefull, the sap of sherry sacke, hunge at his muchato: the top of his nose was sign'd ore with the *English* malt. . . . Red strossers, and a blew codpiece garded with yellow, like the tags of a jackalant's jerkin, his gowne under one arme. . . . His gate was sprightly, his habit anticke, and his gesture apish and peart.[2]

This type of Coney-catcher was as stale as Sir Oliver Anchovy's perfumed jerkin, and had been fully described by John Awdeley. He had to be jovial in appearance, dressed in the latest fashion as a toper and boon companion; for it was on his fine clothes and ready address that his livelihood depended. Walking the streets of London in broad daylight, he would be, like Master Shift, of that admirable and happy memory which could accost as an old friend any rich and benevolent Gull who might cross his path. He would launch into a long tale of misfortune and be very embarrassed and perhaps a

---

[1] R. Dixon, *Canidia*, 1683, IV, viii, 46.
[2] *Scourge of Corruption*, 1615, B2.

little indignant at being offered a groat, but (with some apt allusion to Horace) would eventually conquer his scruples. At the same time he would protest that what he wanted was not casual charity but a loan or some sort of employment. "Therefore, good syr," he would say smilingly, "as you seeme to be a handsome man your selfe, and also such a one as pitieth the miserable case of handsome men, as now your eyes and countenance showeth to have some pitie upon this my miserable complaint . . ."[1] by which time the Gull would have been unable to resist so powerful an *argumentum ad hominem*, and have parted with a gold angel.

The first duty of the Coney-catcher was to learn this art of wheedling, "a subtle Insinuation into the Humours, Inclinations, Natures, and Capacitie" of their victims. There were many lesser types of Courtesy Man. There was the Faungest, who discovered the names of some rich person's relatives and various particulars of his home and early life, and then would accost him in the street, saying he had just met his sister, or old George, or some other among the Gull's acquaintances. This shift seldom gained more than a free drink at the nearest tavern, but always that, even if the Faungest had to suggest it. Then he would fumble with his purse strings till the Gull paid, cry out that it was on him, and then (easily persuaded) shrug his shoulders and yield with excellent grace.

Other Courtesy Men aimed higher. There were thousands of simple country squires and wealthy undergraduates who wanted to be in the Italianate

[1] Awdeley, *Fraternity of Vagabonds*, E.E.T.S., p. 7.

L

fashion and gain a little polish abroad. It would
not be long before such a green-witted gallant met
casually in the street with a charming and cultured
gentleman who had been travelling for years and
was anxious to go abroad again, though he could
not find a suitable companion. To be quite candid
also—money was a bit tight these days. The rest
followed inevitably.

> Then this Gull-groper doth most craftily
> Intrude himself into the company
> Of this same woodcock, and he doth pretend
> Himself to be to him a cordial friend. . . .
> And when he hath a fit occasion caught,
> As at an Ale-house over a morning's draught,
> His mind he breaks . . .[1]

suggesting, perhaps, a marriage with some rich
heiress or a trip to Italy. If the Gull agrees, the
Courtesy Man insists on making all preparations
for the voyage, and the Gull is persuaded to hand
over cash in advance, which he never sees again.

No young gallant could stroll about London without
being followed by a horde of Courtesy Men, eager to
try their skill.

> Like his shaddowe they will never be from his heeles, but
> dogge him into what place soever hee goes, especially if
> hee bee a young country-gentleman whom his father hath
> sent up to the City to see fashions. . . . He shall not go
> into a Taverne, Ordinarie (or almost any friend's house)
> but they will be as nigh his body as his sinnes are his soule,
> and by some sinister way, sement and glue themselves into
> his familiaritie whatsoever it cost them.[2]

---

[1] *Alazono-Mastix*, 1651, p. 10.
[2] W. Fennor, *The Compters Commonwealth*, 1617, p. 30.

General warrants, mentioning no one by name but empowering the holder to arrest any whom he suspected, were often issued by Justices. This illegal practice was the cause of a flourishing minor branch of Coney-catching. If any citizen had his purse stolen, the Coney-catcher would hear of it through members of his organization, go to the victim of the cut-purse and offer to help him to regain his property for a few shillings. He then obtained a warrant from the Justice and black-mailed a few old gaolbirds or innocent conies by threatening them with arrest. Sometimes they actually went as far as to arrest half a dozen shady characters and send them to Newgate, afterwards agreeing to say no more against them, on receipt of a small sum.

More important than such small deer was the Ring Faller. This trick had been performed in Luther's day by the Wiltners. It consisted in obtaining a number of "fayre copper rings" and dropping them along the street like bait. When someone picked up one of these, the Ring Faller was immediately at hand, claiming to have seen it first and demanding his share. After an amicable argument he would generously agree to be content with a few shillings. His reluctance to part with the ring and its apparent value naturally had the effect of raising the price. The device was employed through-out the eighteenth century, and was known then as Cross-dropping. In 1796 a Cambridge ironmonger met a man named Hodges. They walked together idly chatting along Portugal Street, when Hodges suddenly stopped and pointed to a parcel by the pavement. In it they found a diamond cross with a receipt for £320. Hodges persuaded the ironmonger to keep the cross till he could communicate with the police, and accepted a bill of £100 as surety, with half a crown of which he bought a new and still brighter cross.

It was money easily gained, when the trick was successful; but all these were tricks not too often to be played. Nor did these stray roaming cheats belong to the inner circle of the Coney-catchers' fraternity.

X

THE LAWS OF THE CONEY-CATCHERS

"By a multitude of hateful rules," says Greene, "they exercise their villanies." The complicated system of Coney-catching laws was enshrined in no statute book, nor is it easy to tell where truth ends and the towering fabrications of the journalists begin. According to the pamphleteers each cheating device was called a Law, and practised by a small group of professionals and experts. There were more than thirty different methods of groping the Gull— there were certainly thirty variously named "Laws"— but of these four or five stand out above the rest. It is astonishing how many tricks were invented by the Coney-catchers. There was a small group of men who devoted themselves to the stealing and re-selling of horses; others, working in pairs, practised the Lifting Law—absconding in a series of subtle and elaborate moves with goods from the mercers' or goldsmiths' shops. There were the King's Takers, who pilfered from pedlar's trays, and the Heavers, who filched books from roadside stalls. There were the Five Jumps at Leapfrog, each of which was practised by a special company. The "Second Jump" was a not very ingenious method of getting bed and board at an inn without having to pay for it. The third was practised by the Faungests: the fifth was the cozening of the cheapjack at a fair, who brandishes tin spoons and sells them as silver ones. Every nefarious activity of man seems to have had its corresponding "Law."

One of the more curious, and now wholly obsolete, Laws was that of the Falconers. Falconers worked in pairs. Acting as master and servant, they would ride boldly up to the door of some impressive mansion, and call for the squire. When the owner of the house appeared, the Coney-catcher would say, "Sir, I am a poore Scholar, and the report of your vertues hath drawne me hither, venturously bold, to fixe your worthy name as a patronage to a poore short discourse which here I dedicate (out of my love) to your noble and eternall memory."[1] Few country worthies could resist such a chance of seeing their names in print, and four or five gold pieces would be eagerly produced. The Falconers then repaired to some neighbouring house and repeated the trick. A most witty, smooth and damnable conveyance.

The Jacks of the Clock House, who took their name from the figures on Paul's clock, were forgers of a like nature. They sold other men's ballads, or attached sham dedications to books, in return for a fee. There is here, no doubt, an explanation of the fulsome absurdity of many of the Elizabethan dedications. The custom became a polite form of brigandage. It towered to fantastic heights. Markham's *Cavalrice* has eight addresses; Thomas Fuller embellished his Church History with more than sixty. Like a Barker at a Fair he cries his wares and shamelessly hands round the hat. What Doctor Johnson thunderously calls the "meanness and servility of hyperbolical adulation" owed not a little to these counterfeit authors.

There was also the Curber's Law. One stole down

---

[1] Dekker, *Lanthorne & Candle-light*, p. 220 (Temple ed.).

twilit streets bearing a large iron hook, and put it through various windows, pulling forth what one could. The Curber's Law had been adopted by the Coney-catchers from the old beggars' order of Hookers or Anglers. These men had been furnished with a stick six feet long, jointed like a fishing-rod, with a small hole bored through it about an inch from the top. Through this hole they inserted an iron hook; and would then creep down the dark street, leaving a Watcher at the corner, and spy out any fat snappings or windows carelessly left ajar. They stood below in the road, poking through the open window with their hooks, like children at a twopenny dip; with dire results now and then, as Ned Browne testified.

A little later the Curber became known as the Budge. But by that time it was rather more difficult to stand in the road unobserved, bearing a fishing-rod and poking from window to window. The Budge was the man who slipped into a house in the dark and snatched up cloaks and valuables as they came to hand. It was scarcely so romantic an occupation as it had once been; and when Blear-eyed Moll accused Booth of being a "sneaking Budge-rascal," the word had become a cant term for a casual pilferer. His associate, the Snudge, used to enter a house during the day and conceal himself under the bed of the unwary householder.

> The Budge it is a delicate trade,
>   And a delicate trade of fame;
> For when that we have bit the bloe,[1]
>   We carry away the game.[2]

[1] Done the job.　　　　[2] J. Shirley, *Triumph of Wit*, 1724, p. 154.

The easiest and commonest method of trapping the Gull was by suggesting a game of dice or cards at a tavern. Gambling was one of the accomplishments of the complete gentleman; the Fastidious Brisks of the day were as easily rooked at the card tables as the Stephens were pick-pocketed in the market-place. Certainly gambling was as much the conventional equipment of the man of fashion as the ability to sing, to play the lute or to pen woeful ballads made to his mistress's eyebrow. "If he can dice, playe, and daunce, hee is named a proper and a fine nimble man: if he wil loiter and live idly upon other mens labours, and sit all day and night at cards and dice, he is named a good companion." It is a common complaint that anyone who cannot play "post, cente, gleke, or such other games" is known as a Lobbe and a Clown; and some writers put it down to careless upbringing on the part of the parents, others, curiously, to the "hope of a long life" which thus defers the day of repentance.[1] The young man eager to do the right thing was easy game. Very often, we are told, the Gull—even though he realized he was being robbed—would make no resistance, merely because of the humiliation of confessing his gullibility.

In a dialogue between two citizens, R. and M., Gilbert Walker reveals the common method of attack. R. describes how, wandering one day about Paul's, he noticed a gentleman "fair dressed in silks, gold, and jewels, with three or four servants in gay liveries." This impressive stranger, after watching R. for some time, at last approached him, com-

[1] J. Northbrooke, *Treatise Against Dicing, Dauncing, etc.*, 1577.

mented on his dismal looks and suggested that he
should forget his troubles in a little merry entertainment. R. was charmed by his companion's courtesy
and impressed by such a display of wealth; and
they went arm in arm together down the street.
When they came to the stranger's house, they found
dinner laid on a fair diaper cloth, and three or four
other distinguished-looking men present. At the
end of the meal the servants came in with a silver
bowl full of dice and cards and they sat down to
an afternoon's play; at which R. sped not so well
as he would wish. It was not till he had lost all his
money that he realized he had fallen into the hands
of a gang of professional gamblers.[1]

Dicing was a very common amusement of the time,
and many, virtuously given as a gentleman need
be, played, like Falstaff, "not above seven times
a week." Passing any tavern window, you could
have seen a little company bowed, mute and intent,
over a game of Mumchance. Fragments of their
conversation would float into the street—

Look ye, to make us merrier, who comes here?
A fresh gamester? Master Bubble, God save you.
Tu quoque . . .
Come, gentlemen, here's dice . . .
I have the dice; set, gentlemen. . . . For me, six.
And six that.
Nine: One, two, three, four, five, six, seven, and eight:
eighteen shillings.
What's yours, sir?
Mine's a baker's dozen.[2]

---

[1] *A Manifest Detection of Dice Play*, 1532, p. 11.
[2] John Cooke, *Greenes Tu Quoque, or the Cittie Gallant*, 1614. (In Dodsley's *Old Plays*, XI, pp. 216-223.)

Here was the Coney-catcher's excellent opportunity. Many diced for pleasure; but the Ordinaries were always crowded with those Sir Revells who made it their chief profession in life. Every gaming table was surrounded by these sharks and by their desperate victims, staking all they had on their last throw. Nothing could save them, if they lost, from beggary or from turning Coney-catchers themselves and risking the gallows. Duels were fought daily over the cards or the dice; there were scenes of violence and despair. A dreadful fate befell one lustie ladde named Siquila, who, losing his money at one throw, blasphemed and swore and cried aloud, "If I had the Divell here, I would eat him!" No sooner had he spoken these words than "A Spider (or else the Divel in the likenesse of a Spider) came down over his mouth; which, as soon as he sawe, he snatcht into his mouth, and so died presently."[1]

To the puritans of the time this was no excessive punishment for the sin of adding blasphemy to gaming. The dice had long been symbols of viciousness and prodigality. They had been made originally of the bones of a witch, and her skin had been fashioned into the first Court card. According to Bishop Babington, the Devil had been the discoverer of the game. According to another writer, the Court cards were the pictures of forgotten pagan gods and goddesses, and a hundred years before the pulpit had discovered no less than nine individual and damnable sins in the throwing of a die.

For this "detestable privy robbery" had become an art, and the methods of the Coney-catchers grew

[1] *Siquila*, 1587, p. 77.

daily more cunning and elaborate. Dicing and
gambling had become Laws among the fraternity.
"For the obtaining of this skill (of filthie dice-playing)"
says Northbrook in his splenetic little treatise, "they
have made it as it were an arte, and have their
peculiar termes for it; and a number of lewde persons
have, and daily doe apply it . . . when they associate
together with their . . . fellowe theeves." There
were regiments and officers, according to Dekker, in
this "battle between folly and sophistication." They
had their headquarters at Fulham, which became
so noted for sharpers that a Fullam was a common
synonym for a die. Like the beggars, the Dicers
followed certain laws, "giving to divers vile, patching
shifts" that honourable name. The law known as
Gull-groping was a form of usury. The Gull-groper
waited till some young gallant had lost all his money,
and then, while he was still in the heat of play,
stepped forward and offered to lend him a few hundred
pounds on a bond of repayment. But the chief of
their devices was the Cheting Law—a beggar's
word—a law which depended for its success on the
use of various subtly modelled dice. Dekker gives a
list of fourteen different false dice used by the Chetor,
chief among which was the Langret, "a well-favoured
die that seemeth good and square, yet is the forehead
longer on the cater and tray than any other."[1]
The substitution of the false die for the true was a
trick requiring some skill, and had originally been
the art of the Foist, whose hands had become nimble
through long practice in other people's pockets.
"What shifts," asks R. in Walker's dialogue, "have

[1] Walker, *Manifest Detection*, p. 24.

they to bring this false die in and out?" "A jolly
fine shift," replies M., "that properly is called
foisting."

Some dice were delicately treated with hair and
quicksilver; others were dropped on the floor as
the true die fell, and rapidly exchanged. "I trowe,"
says Ascham, "there is not halfe so muche crafte
used in no one thinge in the worlde, as in this cursed
thynge." If the game happened to be going badly
with the Coney-catchers, in spite of their tricks, then
they would turn on the unhappy Gull and accuse
him of using false dice, hiding the true ones in their
hands and demanding their money back.

These Chetors and Shifters were well known.
In a pamphlet called *Look on me, London*, a countryman
warns his son against these dicing gangs, mentioning
the names of money-brokers and cursing the gaming-
house where "cogging knaves win more money
in an howre, than many an honest man spendeth
in one yeare." And Edward Underhill, the Hot
Gospeller, as early as 1553 made a list of the most
notorious dicers of his day. Banbery, Dapers, Morgan
of Salisbury Court, Lusty Young had all perished;
but they had handed on their skill to the Bob Wedens
of a later day. Every adept had a group of eager
and impoverished scholars about him, ruined gallants
for the most part, who found Coney-catching the
only way to escape gathering the wind to beggar's
haven.

To Roger Ascham and most of the writers of the
age, cards were the Green Pathway to hell, whereby
followed a hundred gowtie, dropsy diseases. Scarcely
one poor countryman could come to London without

meeting a charming friend of one of his relatives, eager to have a casual game of Gleek or Noddy.

> *Item*, that I met withall
> a very loving Cosen,
> who needs would be of my Countrey,
> and gave me halfe a dozen;
> and at the last a pare of Cards
> they cunningly did bring in;
> I will not say what they made me pay,
> but Ile whistle instead of singing.[1]

Drunken Barnaby was cheated at Hoxton; Croydon and Romford were towns well known for card-sharpers, who would travel in the disguise of serving-men when their faces became too familiar to Londoners.

Their procedure in town or country was invariably the same, whether they called themselves Rooks, Pads, Biters, or Coney-catchers; whether their victims were Gulls, Lambs, or Conies. They smiled at each other when their victim was fleeced, saying, "The Lamb is bitten"; and when he entered the Den, if they thought him a sure Bubble, they would begin by losing small sums to increase his confidence.

Their favourite game was Primero, in which Queen Elizabeth delighted; and the numberless "Laws" which they followed were not yet staled by time. They pinched the cards privily with their nails; or turned up the corners of the aces. They laid a "bumbe carde finely under, over, or in the middes, &c. and what not."[2] They marked the backs of them with ink; they had cunningly arranged mirrors; or they sat with a demure seamstress, who flashed signals with her knitting-needles. Reginald Scot warns

[1] *Roxburghe Ballads*, II, p. 83.   [2] Northbrook, *Treatise*, p. 142.

the coney to beware of him that seems simple or drunken, and particularly of any bystander that stands idly watching the game. Indeed, the commonest method of approach was to make the coney think that they were conies themselves, and to lead him on by playing on his vanity.

The favourite law was that known as Barnard's. This required four players and a Gull. The players were called the Taker-up, the Verser, the Barnard, and the Rutter.

The Taker-up was a man of some culture, whose special gift was the ability to talk charmingly on every subject under the sun. Seeing a Gull just down from the country, with a bung full of gold, he led him into conversation, at the end of which "it shall 'scape him hardly but he will be that Gull's countryman at least."[1] The second act brought the Gull to the nearest tavern, rather proud of his new friend. There they met with the Verser, very grave and richly dressed, representing a landed proprietor. After a few genial words had passed between these three, the Barnard stumbled in, scattering gold and apparently dead drunk, "lined with money and malmsey." He flung guineas about the room to create confidence and to show that he had no objection to losing a few. Cards were brought in, and, after being allowed to win enough to make him reckless, the Gull was handsomely fleeced. Should he show any signs of resentment, there was the Rutter standing with drawn sword in the doorway, ready to delay the Gull in a brawl what time the Barnard stole off with his ill-got gains. Barnard's

[1] Greene, *Notable Discovery of Coosnage*, p. 12. (Bodley Head Qtos.)

Law lived long. In a pamphlet of 1770 called *Thieving Detected* it is elaborately described, every move precisely as it had been performed two hundred years before; except that the Taker-up, the Verser, the Barnard, and the Gull are known as the Picker-up, the Kid, the Cap, and the Flat.

Once the coney was trapped the rest was simple. But with Greene and Rowlands and their fellow pamphleteers pouring caveats from the Press, it became no easy matter to persuade a young man to play cards with strangers. Up and down Holborne or Fleet Street or St. Paul's the Coney-catchers would stroll on the look-out for the sight-seeing countryman. "There's a coney!" they would whisper if they saw one pass. Then the Taker-up walked casually to the coney and greeted him—"Sir, God save you, you are welcom to London, how doth all our good friends in the country, I hope they be all in health?" The coney, of course, stared at him blankly, but the Taker insisted that they must somewhere have met, since his face and accent were so familiar. Thus he was soon furnished with the names of the coney's family, the place where he lived and his occupation; and off they went to the tavern to forget their embarrassment over a pot of ale. If the prey was not so easily to be caught, the Taker-up went back and told the Verser all his information; whereupon the Verser tried again, this time well fortified with intimate details of the coney's life and home—

What goodman Barton, how are al our friends about you? You are well met, I have the wine for you, you are welcome to town.[1]

[1] Greene, *Notable Discovery*, p. 19.

He then claimed to be an old friend of one of Master Barton's more distant relatives and offered him a drink to celebrate the happy occasion.

If all else failed there was still a final resort. One of the Coney-catchers went along the road in front of the coney and dropped a shilling on the pavement. The coney inevitably stopped to pick it up, either with the intention of keeping or returning it. But at once the Coney-catcher just at his heels claimed a half share and insisted that he had seen it first. They wrangled pleasantly, and agreed at last to change it at the nearest tavern. It was the old game of the Ring Faller turned to different ends. Once inside the tavern the coney was lost, for the cards were set ready at the table and the Rutter barred his retreat with drawn blade at the doorway.

"What better alective could Satan devise to allure and bring men pleasantly into damnable servitude?"

MOLL FRITH

XI

THE ROARING BOYS

THE Brotherhood of Coney-catchers remained for so long more or less immune that it became conscious of its power. It had started in the early sixteenth century as a number of small, isolated groups of cheaters; by 1600 these formed a powerful body with sanctuaries of vice within the walls of London.

The knowledge of the terror they inspired turned the Coney-catchers from fawning cheats to gangs of disreputable bullies, roaming the streets at night and defying the inefficient and disorganized police. They became Roaring Boys, Bonaventoes, Quarterers, Bravadors. They exercised a kind of mob law of their own, and were the origin of the Scowrers, Nickers, and Mohocks of a later age. They were a heterogeneous company, many of them idle apprentices or gallants sunk deep in debt; and the more uproarious among them found their sole amusement in terrorizing respectable citizens, in taking the wall, in clashing their sabres with a profusion of inkhorn oaths and slitting the noses of the recalcitrant. These debauchees, in an anonymous and violent satire of the time, are said in their "mad and unheard of revels" to pierce their veins and quaff their own blood. They gave themselves the title of Bully, much as the Revolutionaries in France called each other "Citizen." Bully Dawson and Bully Watson, Tom Brown's friend, were two of the last of the tribe.

No Roarer was complete without his long pipe

M

of tobacco, for smoking was then the hallmark of extreme masculinity. Tobacco was supposed to be the smoke that indicated the secret fires of virility—

> Tobacco is a Whyffler,
> And cries huff snuff with furie,
> His pipes, his club and linke,
> He's the wiser that does drinke;
> Thus armed I fear not a furie.
> This makes me sing so ho, so ho, boyes,
>   Ho boyes sound I loudly;
>   Earth nere did breed
>   Such a jovial weed
>   Whereof to boast so proudly.[1]

For a time it had been the privilege of noblemen to smoke; later "every tinker, rogue, scavenger, or hangman" became a devotee to this Devil-wort. It was then that a host of pamphleteers—savagely, as in the *Satires* of Hall—facetiously, as in *Diets Dry Dinner* or *Work for Chimney Sweepers*—academically, as in Vaughan's *Naturall and Artificiall Directions*—attacked the habit. They were headed by the King himself, who compared it to the "Stygian smoke of the pit that is bottomelesse"—but it was not so much the tobacco that roused resentment as the ruffian gangs that were its chief users. These were the Puffers or High Huffers, whose crest and symbol was a pipe, and who were an uproarious offshoot of the Roaring Boys.

Sir Walter Scott describes the typical member of this freemasonry of scoundrels, bullies, cheats, and debtors as a shaggy, uncombed ruffian with enormous moustaches turned back over his ears,

---

[1] B. Holiday, *Marriage of the Arts*, 1618.

puffing at a long pipe and trailing an immense
sabre behind him along the cobbles. They took
refuge for the most part in the grim squalor of Alsatia,
and sallied forth in singing bands at nightfall. They
were bound together under oath to help each other
against their sworn foes the Constable and the
Creditor. This oath of initiation was taken by the
neophyte on a sword hilt, and he was then taught
the elements of the art of Roaring.

Trimtram. Well, you must learn to roar here in London . . .
Chough. How long has roaring been an exercise, thinkest
thou, Trimtram?
Trim. Ever since guns came up; the first was your roaring
Meg.[1]

This art, the origin of which is thus attributed
to Long Meg, was the art of terrifying the Respectable
by loud noises and uncouth words. "He that can
lashe out the bloodiest oathes," says Stubbes, "is
computed the bravest fellowe. . . . It is the signe
of a coragious harte, of a valiaunt stomacke, and of
a generous, heroicall, and puissant minde."

The Roarer was usually to be observed standing
astride a broken chair with a sabre or a tankard
in his hand, searching for someone who had insulted
him. "Let me be torn into mammocks," he would
shout, "with wild bears, if I make not a gallimaufry
of thy heart, and keep thy skull for my quaffing
bowl, you base, cheating slave!"[2] His common
method of addressing the servant of an inn was,
"Damme, we will have more wine, sirrah, or we'll
down into the cellar and drown thee in a butt of

[1] Middleton, *A Fair Quarrel*, II, ii.
[2] John Day, *Blind Beggar of Bednall Green*, 1659, G2.

Malmsey, and hew all the hogsheads in pieces. . . .
By this flesh, let's have wine, or I will cut thy head
off, and have it roasted and eaten . . ."[1] Most of
them were little more formidable than Bobadil,
and shared his habit of telling tremendous stories
of their own courage. They would cover their faces
with strips of black plaster, as if they concealed
the scars of a hundred desperate duels.

Perhaps the Roarer was an inevitable result of
the young extravagance of the Elizabethans. He
was certainly an amusingly familiar sight in tavern
parlours, shaking his fists and shouting his bombastic
tales.

He begins you a story of a Sea Fight; and though he
never were further by water than the *Bear-garden*, or *Cuckolds-
haven*, yet . . . he persuades you himself was present and
performed Miracles; that he waded knee-deep in Blood on
the Upper-Deck, and never thought to serenade his Mistress
so pleasant as the Bullets' Whistling.[2]

Sometimes he recalls Falstaff—

I'll tell you, Sir! My paunch is nothing but a pile of
bullets; when I was in any service I stood between my
general and the shot like a mud wall: I am all lead: from
the crown of the head to the sole of the foot, not a sound
bone about me.[3]

But the Roarers were more like overgrown school-
boys than dangerous crooks. "Why," says Lord
Feesimple, in Field's play, "I will have my humour.
If you love me, let's go break windows somewhere."
The gallants of the Restoration amused themselves

---

[1] N. Field, *Amends for Ladies*, III, iv.
[2] *Character of a Coffee House*, Harl. Misc., VI, 429.
[3] Beaumont & Fletcher, *The Honest Man's Fortune*, II, i.

ROARING BOYS

with the more adult occupation of chasing young
ladies in the parks. They liked to fancy themselves
members of a desperate gang; but in truth there
were Roarers of two very different types. There
were the blustering toughs of Alsatia with cudgels
in their hands and hired bullies at their heels; and
there were the high-spirited youths who were annoyed
by the respectable, and expressed their annoyance
by making a nuisance of themselves in taverns and
twilit streets—

> Domineering, swaggering blades,
>   and cavaliers that flashes——
> That throw the jugs against the walls,
>   and break in pieces glasses.[1]

Their dreaded war-cry, "Sa! Sa!" made many a
Watchman tremble, for beating up the Watch was a
favourite amusement. More delightful still was a
casual encounter with some honest citizen hurrying
home at night by way of the Sanctuary of the Roarers
called "Bermuda." They hated anything that savoured
remotely of respectability, conventionality, or a
reverence for law and order.

> Whateer we get by gulls
> of country or of city,
> old flatcaps or young heirs
> or lawyer's clerks so witty;
> by sailors newly landed
> to put in for fresh waters:
> by wandering gander-mooners[2]

---

[1] *Roxburghe Ballads*, II, p. 32.

[2] A "Gander-Mooner" was their name for the rake who roamed
about twilit fields seeking occasion for debauch while his wife was lying-
in during her "gander month."

> or muffled, late night-walkers,
> with a hone, a hone, a hone,
> no cheaters nor decoys
> shall have a share, but alone
> the bravest Roaring Boys![1]

Later they would inherit the talents so generously left to them by James Hynd in his *Testament*. The Brethren of the Blade would roam St. Martin's Lane and Covent Garden no more; but get their revenge on the law-abiding at the pistol's mouth. Out of the Brotherhood of the Roarers soon developed the last and greatest of the brotherhoods who followed the Highway Law. The reward went to confidence and courage; as for conscience, the case was succinctly stated by the Roaring Boy who met Tom Brown and his Indian at the gaming-table—

Split my windpipe, Sir, you are a fool, and don't understand trap; the whole world's a cheat.[2]

Most famous of the Roarers was Mary Frith, merry Moll Cutpurse of the Bankside. The frontispiece of Middleton's *Roaring Girl* shows her dressed in man's clothes, with a sprig of mistletoe in her hat, a huge pipe, a sword and a cloak. She was said to have a voice that could drown all the city, and invariably appeared in male clothes—flatly against Scripture, as Thomas Fuller remarks. Her boisterous masculinity recalls Long Meg of Westminster. Her ill deeds on the road remind one of Anne Bonny who killed a servant with a clasp-knife and fought on the blood-stained quarter-deck of Calico Jack.

"Quaffing one night late at the *Devil* Tavern . . ."

---

[1] Middleton, *A Fair Quarrel*, IV, iv.
[2] T. Brown, *Amusements Serious and Comical*, ch. viii.

Somehow the words create a more vivid picture than anything else in her curious biography.[1] The rafters of the Devil Tavern had rung often enough to her oaths. She was more aggressively male than any man, and her contemporaries suggested more than once that Mistress Hic and Haec was a hermaphrodite. For a time she was the terror of the streets.

She was born in the Barbican in 1589, and showed early enough by her fondness for boys' games what a Tomrig and Rumpscuttle of a wench she would grow into.

She could not endure the sedentary life of sewing or stitching, a Sampler was as grievous as a winding sheete, her Needle, Bodkin and Thimble, she could not think on quietly; wishing them changed into sword and Dagger for a bout at Cudgels.[2]

At a precocious age she learnt to swear astonishing oaths, and never had any truck with the magpie chat of the wenches. A good mastiff was the only thing she joyed in; and by the time she was fifteen or so, she first put on man's clothes and decided to "Live by the quick." During her wild youth she had made friends with pedlars, fortune-tellers and various London Coney-catchers; and she found no difficulty in becoming a receiver of stolen goods. A receiver had a certain power of blackmail in the underworld—a power that Jonathan Wild afterwards exploited to the full—and it was thus that Moll Cutpurse laid the foundations of her empire over the Coney-catchers. In her diary she points out that

[1] *Life and Death of Mrs. Mary Frith*, 1662.
[2] *Life and Death of Mrs. Frith*, p. 6.

the world is made up of Cheaters and Cheatees, and decides that she may as well belong to the more profitable company of the two.

Her father, a respectable shoemaker, was not unnaturally alarmed by Moll's behaviour and appearance. Her relatives determined to get rid of her and pack her off to Virginia. She was then just twenty and still woman enough, they thought, for some Jack of the New World to marry. She was lured, under pretence of visiting a Fair, down to Gravesend, and there clapped under the hatches of an outward-bound ship. The captain, however, was tender-hearted and let her escape.

This incident was the turning-point in her career; for at once she became a full-fledged member of the Brotherhood of Coney-catchers in the capacity of receiver. They would not allow her to train as a Foist. The Brotherhood "hates a Bungler as much as a Dunce," and Moll lacked the long middle finger which is essential to the expert Foist.

She established a kind of Clearing House for stolen goods next door to the Globe Tavern in Fleet Street. Here thieves brought their booty and here too owners came to recover them, Moll and the Cutpurses sharing the rewards of the spoils. She thus not only gathered a knowledge of the underworld as wide and as exact as Jonathan Wild's, but became the acknowledged head of a great gang of bullying cheats and robbers. "The Boyes," she called them. They would obey her slightest wish, and followed her like a bodyguard as she paced down Fleet Street in top-boots, puffing at her long pipe and swinging her sabre.

It was not long before she was arrested. An officious Constable of the Watch hauled her to Newgate under a charge of "unreasonable and suspitious walking." She was released with a small fine and an insatiable thirst for vengeance. She sent one of the "imps of her thieves' battalion" as a messenger to the constable who had arrested her, with the news that an uncle had died and left the constable all his money. The simple-minded man fell into the trap and was led by Moll's messenger over the country-side to Shropshire, where he was given the slip and left to meditate on the rewards of *hubris*. Moll was in and out of the courts. Arraigned for being a Receiver, she ordered her chief Foist to pick the pocket of the judge, and remove the evidence. Again and again she escaped punishment. But on one occasion she was compelled to do penance in a white sheet at St. Paul's for "wearing undecent and manly apparel." She turned this to excellent use. While the crowds were gaping at her and throwing their missiles, the Boyes were passing quietly round from pocket to pocket.

It was about this time that Moll was rumoured to have married the curious hermaphrodite known as Anniseed-Water Robin. She is known, however, to have quarrelled with the creature and set the Boyes to throw darts at him and drive him from her door. Moreover Anniseed-Water Robin was at that time the wife of Jack Cottington, *alias* Mulled Sack, one of the most outrageous members of Moll's gang, who had won a legendary fame for standing in the pillory with a tinker's kettle on his head. Moll had met with this eccentric chimney-sweeper at the Devil

Tavern, where he had become a champion drinker of sack. Anniseed Robin soon drove him back to his Rhenish, and he associated with the Five Women Barbers of Drury Lane, women as well known in their professions as Moll was in hers—

> Did yee ever heare the like,
> Or ever heare the same,
> Of five woemen-barbers
> That liv'd in Drewry Lane?[1]

He had joined Moll's gang and became the most expert of her Foists, making a speciality of robbing the congregations of London churches. His disguises were so subtle and so numerous that only the long pipe he invariably smoked betrayed his identity. When he became King of the Beggars, he founded a school for young thieves and would give demonstrations in the art of picking pockets, passing like an itinerant conjurer from one tavern to another. He was nearly hanged for stealing from the greatcoat of Oliver Cromwell later in his life, and was forced to flee to Cologne. There he robbed Charles the Second of £1500. He returned eventually to London to try and exchange some secret documents which he did not possess for his freedom, which he did not possess either. He was very properly executed at Smithfield in 1659.

Meanwhile Moll had fallen from her high station. She began keeping a little zoo of dogs and parrots which she would put to bed every night, covering them with sheets and blankets. She was always surrounded by her famous bull-dogs, and carried a "good Batton" in her hand to keep them in order

[1] Quoted by Aubrey, *Brief Lives*, II, p. 73.

or to crack the heads of her enemies. Her business as a Receiver languished, but she gained a certain amount of favour in the eyes of the authorities by supplying the conduit of Fleet Street with wine at the celebration of Charles the First's return from Scotland. On that occasion she interrupted the procession by rushing forward and grasping the royal hand. "Welcome home, Charles!" she bellowed jovially at him.

But she was no longer "Queen regent of Misrule." She resigned from active service in the underworld and entered the contemplative life, playing with her collection of baboons, squirrels, dogs, and parrots. She amused herself also by sewing and singing, though she confessed she had a voice "as gratefull to the Ears of people, as the squeak of a Mandrake at its Revulsion." At the age of seventy she died of the dropsy. "I expect not," she said, "nor will I purchase a Funerall Commendation; but . . . let the *Sexton* mumble Two or Three Dusty Claiy words and put me in, and there's an end."

There was an end, indeed; for by the time she died her reputation had been forgotten and the plays of the old dramatists were no longer on the stage. There was no one left to write her epitaph for her: but she had written her own long ago—

"I was always a good *Fellow*, and loved good *Liquor*."

PART THREE

THE DECLINE OF THE BROTHERHOODS

XII

THE LAST OF THE BEGGARS

ON October 29, 1618, the last of the proud gay lords of Elizabeth was murdered on the scaffold. The end of the golden age had come, and with it the disbanding of the Beggars' Brotherhood. The causes which had led to their increase no longer existed; the warfare, though not near its end, was already waged against defeated forces. The machinery of Justice and repression became more and more efficient, so that the roadside tramp was transformed from a recruit in a formidable army to a solitary and miserable wayfarer. Most of his fellows became at length respectable citizens, fought in the Civil War, or founded families among the remote plantations. Some pursued their trade in a different guise, and took to the high-road, no longer begging for money but demanding it at the pistol's mouth. The efficiency of the police was slowly increasing; and Edward Hemings's patent for lighting the city was a powerful discouragement to the night-hawks of the Restoration. Moreover, in these Tickle Times there was a certain indisposition to part readily with money. King James gave the last kick to the corpse, branding all rogues on the shoulder with a great Roman R, and packing them off to the plantations of Virginia. "From the crowded crossing, from the corners of streets and turnings of alleys, the parting Genius of Beggary" was with sighing sent. In 1633 the Inns of Court entertained Charles the First on his return from Scotland with a Masquerade. The Antimasque was much appreciated. It showed an army of sham beggars mounted on the sorriest jades and playing discordant music on tongs and keys. It is a grimly ironical commentary on a menace that had so far disappeared as to be taken for a jest.

The further history of the beggars is no longer the history of a number of elaborate organizations, but of isolated evildoers, solitary, hunted, formidable men, who owed service to no one and were the enemies of all. The wheel had come full circle; and the beggar had returned to the condition of the wandering outlaw of the Middle Ages. There was nothing of the old sharing of spoils; no longer did the experts of the trade hint their secrets to the neophyte, tipping the immemorial wink; and there is a certain regrettable lack of *esprit de corps* in the lives of Jack Sheppard and Major Clancie.

Gangs lingered on, here and there in remoter spots. There was the famous clan of John Gregg, composed entirely of his relatives, living together "in a cave near to the sea-side, in Chovaly in Devonshire." For twenty-five years they prospered by organized robbery. Everyone they robbed they murdered; and everyone they murdered they devoured. Over a thousand victims, according to the chronicler, furnished these Neronian banquets, before two bloodhounds revealed their hiding-place to the constables. Gregg and his wife, together with fourteen children and thirty two grandchildren, were burned alive on the same pyre.

But such ogres were happily rare. England,

according to Bunyan, was shaking and tottering by reason of the burden laid so wickedly upon it by Mr. Badman and his friends. But Mr. Badman was no leader of brotherhoods; he was a mere cheat, a dishonest merchant, who made his living by a subtle process of borrowing and going bankrupt and borrowing again. There was, and will be, plenty of room for Mr. Badman under any government.

The gangs of the beggars had said farewell to their prime. Such brotherhoods that still existed were loose and transitory confederacies. One curious little offshoot was called the Black Guard. This was a swarm of boy-beggars who haunted the courts and kitchens of the big houses and marched with a kind of rough discipline about the London streets. They were amateur Roarers, who took mischievous delight in ramming their links in the faces of benighted wayfarers. Against these lewd and loose fellows and masterless rogues there was a proclamation of the Lord Steward's Office in 1683; and thereafter they vanished, leaving no ripple behind, save a new word for the polite vocabulary.

But there may exist some ground of fact behind the tissue of plagiarisms that forms the Life of Meriton Latroon.

How far Meriton Latroon was a portrait of his author, Richard Head, it is difficult to say. Head, according to Aubrey, "looked like a knave with his gogling eies," but he was indignant at having the book spoken of as his autobiography. *The English Rogue* is a piece of hack journalism, but the earlier chapters were true enough to life. Meriton Latroon, the disruputable hero of the tale, is no longer a

N

member of the ragged and uproarious fraternity.
The frontispiece to the edition of 1665 shows a
magnificent cavalier with a drawn sword and a mask.
"Dam-me your Purse you Rouge," floats in a coloured
scroll from his lips. From the mouth of the trembling
traveller opposite a similar scroll utters, "Save my
life and take all I have." Other wind-swept gon-
falons remark at random, "Cleave his head downe."
"Pricke ye Rascals forwarde." "The Coast is cleare."

The Highway Law was already in full force—the
"Law" of the masked robbers. But, born in due
time, Head might have proved a worthy member of
the Brotherhood. His first deed, at the age of five,
was the murder of a turkey, "which exasperated
his budding passion." He fell in with a master-
beggar, a Prince of Prigs, and together they plied
a roaring trade by hiring stray children to act as
their poverty-stricken family. He became a Curber,
and tramped the streets furtively at twilight with
the peculiar pole that was the symbol of their trade.
He thieved successfully among the markets by throwing
crowds into confusion, casting lighted "crackers and
serpents" among them and running off with dropped
purses. He employed his rare leisure in kicking the
lanterns of the Watch about the streets. After a
brief while he turned into a mere wandering knave-
like Lazarillo or Gil Blas, having adventures sus-
piciously similar to theirs; and when finally he set
sail for Siam and the East Indies, we are nearer
the romances of Defoe than the age of Elizabeth
or James.

Meriton Latroon is Mr. Badman writ large, a
shadowy villain more than half created from old

legends. All this, the "merry jests" and the Rabelaisian adventures, are Mumbo Jumbo, nursery games, compared to the deeds of the dead Brotherhood. They remind one of the benignant witches one sees riding on broomsticks in the moonlight, high above the dark forests where their ancestral grandams squat in hideous communion with the Prince of Darkness. The picture of the Extravagant Prentices with their Lasses at a Taverne Frollick shows a mob of overdressed, excited youths, smoking, drinking and playing dice. The society of thieves has given place to a group of rowdy apprentices, playing jests which irritate rather than alarm the people on whom they prey.

Meriton Latroon was the forerunner of a more famous and more historical personage, the Last of the Beggars, Bampfylde-Moore Carew.

Mr. Carew seems to have possessed many of the talents of his great predecessors. It was the age in which he lived, rather than any deficiency in himself, which lends a certain strain of meanness to his knaveries, and deprives him of the sublime squalor of the Elizabethans. He was born in 1693; and thus passed most of the earlier part of his life in the sober reign of Anne. As a boy he was remarkable for his learning and his adventurous spirits, and his relatives hoped that such qualities would render him an ornament to the Church. It was not long, however, before he fell into the hands of one of those diminished companies of Maunders that still lingered in the remoter countrysides. Into their sorry fellowship he was initiated with some pomp.

A comparison of this initiation ceremony with

the mellow Elizabethan ritual described by Dekker shows how far respectability had encroached on the old lawlessness. In the place of the "booze and belly-cheer" of a century before, the tankards of Huffcap or Father Whoreson, as they affectionately nicknamed their potent liquors, now "nothing is reckoned more infamous than to appear intoxicated during the time of an election." Instead of the stupendous oaths and the upturning of the gage of ale, there is merely a chest with a hole in the lid, like a missionary box. The electors dropped white balls into the box for those they favoured, and black for those they condemned. So closely had the Brotherhood of Beggars come to resemble a literary society! Indeed, the last relic of the old, mad revels, the flying skirts of the Doxy, the Bawdybasket clapping her dionysiac tambourine, was the Ode which the electors chanted in sober unison:

> Cast your nabs and cares away,
> This is Maunder's Holiday;
> In the world look out and see
> Where so happy a King as he?
>
> At the crowning of our King
> Thus we ever dance and sing:
> Where's the nation lives so free
> And so merrily as we?

which resembles nothing so much as some of the more austere of the Presbyterian hymns.

The gang to which Carew belonged had its head-quarters in Lewkenor's Lane, the haunt of cut-purses and a notable nursery of rogues. Here lived Tom Dennis, the hangman; here also the ugliest knave in London, John Smith, who was known as Buckhorse, and chiefly remarkable for his skill as a boxer and a peculiar whistling noise he could make by pressing his fist against his chin. But it was a sorry, ill-disciplined rabble, and Carew himself was more of a travelling conjurer than a true beggar. He was a charlatan who disguised himself and shamelessly screwed money from his friends. He tried every trick known to the trade. He "equipped himself with an old pair of Trowsers" and acted as a Whip-Jack or shipwrecked sailor. He dressed up "as one who had exercised for many years the sacred office of a clergyman at Aberustuth," wearing a large white wig and pacing the streets muttering orisons. Every action revealed the distressed gentleman, too courteous to beg and too hungry to refrain from begging. Like the Courtesy Man of Awdeley's day, any subscription that was too small he at first pretended to reject, only accepting it after embarrassed apologies and a struggle with his sense of honour painful to witness. He acted also as a palliard, tying up one of his legs behind him and, like Ned Browne of old, wearing a "venerable and pity-moving beard." In this way he performed so many notable cozenings that he was elected King of the Beggars in the place of the great Clause Patch—only to be immediately apprehended by a magistrate—

So sudden are the vicissitudes of life! and misfortune springs as it were out of the earth. Thus sudden and unexpected fell the mighty Caesar, the master of the world: and just so frightened Priam looked when the shade of Hector drew his curtains and told him that his Troy was taken.[1]

[1] *Life, Voyages and Adventures of Bampfylde-Moore Carew,* 1768, p. 65.

That was the beginning of his travels, for he was then shipped, like of one Defoe's heroes, off to America, and only returned after a series of hairbreadth escapes. Immediately on landing in England he shaved off his beard, dressed up as an old lady and rushed into the house of Sir Thomas Carew,

acting like a mad woman, beating his head against the wall, kissing his dog and demanding his rent. At last comes one of the women servants, saying, Lady, you are welcome to your rent, and gave him half a crown; but he was not be got rid of so easily, for now he fell a-raving again, and demanded some merry-go-down; upon which they brought him some ale, which he having drunk, took his leave, thanking them with a very low curtsey.[1]

It was not surprising that he should soon have been transported for yet another voyage to America, where he was fortunate enough to meet a friend who offered to pay for his release. Carew's sense of honour only allowed him to accept this after a long struggle, and reluctantly he returned to freedom and his native land. Here he immediately cheated two elderly ladies and a clergyman. Perhaps the most successful and daring of his exploits was performed in Edinburgh. There he pretended to be a madman, and, meeting one of the dignitaries of the Church walking down "Castle Street," he flung his arms about him and insisted on being told who was the father of the Morning Star. His curiosity was only appeased by substantial hush-money.

Another method of earning a living was peculiar to Carew. He used to prowl about churchyards meditatively, in the disguise of a clergyman, reading

[1] *Life and Adventures*, p. 120.

the inscriptions on the tombstones. Whenever he
came upon the grave of someone whose life appeared
to have been more than usually exemplary, he would
seek out the relatives, in the hope that they might
have inherited some of the virtues of the deceased.
If his hopes were justified he would claim a remote
kinship.

But it was not to last long. The end of the Elizabethan Mumper had been starvation in a garret
or keeping sheep by moonlight. Carew was more
fortunate. He happened to enter a church in the
dress of a Counterfeit Crank, and heard a "Right
Reverend Bishop" preach on the text "To those
to whom much is given, much will be required."
Carew was so unpleasantly impressed with these
words that without more ado he resigned the King-
ship of the Beggars, "retired in the western parts to
a neat purchase he had made: and there ended his
days, beloved and respected by all." The last months
of his life he spent in dictating the story of his adventures to a lady named Mrs. Goadby, and the book
became a best-seller in the latter half of the eighteenth
century.

Carew is the last and most famous of the members
of the Beggars' Brotherhood, and he lived at the
very end of its power. There were to be no more
meetings on moonlit heaths or boozings in nocturnal
tippling kens. The company had been broken, and
the stray survivors wandered abroad, begging on
their own. The eighteenth century beggar, even in
Carew's day, had already become that type of mumper
without tradition or pride, over which Elia sheds
his sentimental tear; the kind of Tramp that the Man

of Feeling met and mingled his sobs with on the road to London. The terror and burden of society had become a casual nuisance of the streets, and was soon to be surrounded by the sensibility and sentimentality of a school of minor novelists.

XIII

THE HIGHWAYMEN

MAN is a gregarious animal, and tends always to hunt in flocks. The herd-instinct gathers all members of a clan together in one gigantic multitude, united for the common purpose of preserving one another from extinction. The survival of the fittest never means the survival of the individual; it means the survival of those who can most easily and rapidly conform to the pattern of the tribe.

Thus, criminals, like members of any other profession, may begin as solitary artists, but they will end by joining in some way with their fellows. Otherwise they perish, as the Brotherhood of Beggars perished, once the links that united it had weakened. The gang-making instinct is as old as man. And so, because it gave solidarity and power, the criminal and the tramp tended to join with other criminals and tramps, to invent passwords, to speak secret languages. The stray pedlars and pardoners on the roads of the Middle Ages gradually coalesced into a series of European gangs which terrorized every government of the sixteenth century. If a man lives alone, he becomes either a beast or a god. There were a few of these Aristotelian beasts among the beggars; but they became more and more rare as the Brotherhood increased in power.

By the middle of the seventeenth century the Brotherhood of Beggars had been disbanded. The old tricks had become so well known that to practise

them was a sure road to the Counter. In a final
flicker of defiance the beggars banded together
under the Highway Law.

Highwaymen had flourished as long as coaches
used the roads. It was chiefly because of the increase
in travelling that they appeared in their gangs as
late as they did. The scourge of the Highway Law
reached its height only in the eighteenth century, the
masked riders were as formidable as their Elizabethan
predecessors, and the "bridle-cull" came to be
regarded as a member of "the first class of theives."
Horace Walpole scarcely dared to stir out of his
house even in daylight, so infested were the roads
with these masked and mounted robbers. Lady
Hertford had been attacked on Hounslow Heath
at three o'clock in the afternoon; Doctor Eliot had
been shot at; the Prime Minister's coach was waylaid; the ladies of the Bedchamber dared not even
visit the Queen at Kew after dusk, and the only
road he could consider safe was the lane between
his house and the river, which was "up to the middle
of the horses in water." It was a panic-stricken
country which could put such an innocent as Master
Humphry Clinker in the dock on suspicion of highway
robbery.

The gangs of highwaymen began with the great
increase in travelling during the seventeenth century,
and only ended in the nineteenth, when the desolate
thickets round London had finally disappeared.
Successive governments paid as much attention
to these robbers as had been paid to the beggars
a hundred years before. Death by hanging was the
highwayman's invariable end. But his rewards mean-

MAUNDERERS ON THE PAD

while were large. At Gadshill, Epping Forest, Royston Downs, or any of the wild common lands like Newmarket or Maidenhead Thicket, bands of robbers twenty or thirty strong would ride alongside the roads, sometimes, like Nevison the Yorkshireman, levying a regular tribute from merchants or cattle-drovers, sometimes attacking the mail-coach or the retinues of great nobles. As of old, they met at the country inns, which kept for two hundred years the evil reputation they had won in Tudor times. Without the assistance of the landlords they could never have attained their position.

Travellers are very apt to call for the landlord to sup with them; and then after supper asking what news concerning the Roadmen, and perhaps telling him what money they have and where they put it . . . and the Road they are going and where they lie the next night, and so on.[1]

Then the landlord, for a percentage of the takings, would repeat the whole of his conversation to the highwayman. Some of the more prominent figures on the roads had a system of espionage among the tapsters, ostlers and servants of the inns along the great desolate high-roads. These men kept them regularly informed of the movements of travellers. It was to one of these inns where they were "winkt at" that the highwaymen rode after the robbery, and here they shared the booty, "not without cheating one another." Several thieves, on retiring from business, set up as pawnbrokers, much as a retired seaman might set up as the keeper of a pub. These shops became regular houses for the receiving of stolen goods. The author of the *Thief-Catcher* suggests

[1] *Discoveries of John Poulter*, 1754, p. 38.

that the only way of ridding the land of the high-waymen was by punishing the innkeepers and stable-men who supplied them with food, information and horses. Once the King's Court was attacked by a company on Hounslow Heath and more than thirty coaches were stopped; and near Waltham Cross there was a kind of village of freebooters who sent a signed cartel of defiance to the Government and caused the cavalry to be mustered against them on the Middlesex roads.

The "Blades and Hocks of the Highway" were an apotheosis of the Nips and Foists; and their organization was still more elaborate. The "politic searching of crafty carriers' packs or ripping up the bowels of wide boots and cloak-bags" was no job for the amateur. There was an involved ceremony of initiation, chiefly concerned with the precautions to be adopted on meeting with a Sergeant. The apprentice had to swear

> That if misfortune in your traffic doe
> Betray you to the law, and danger too,
> You must not tell your Complices, nor name
> How by this cursed trade, and life you came;
> If you are pressed hard to particularize,
> Then must you cunningly some names devise . . .
> Now, if you are examined when you fell
> To these lewd courses, then you are to tell
> That you came up here with a full intent
> To goe for service.[1]

Were he taken by the constables, the apprentice had to have a lively and convincing tale ready for them—that he had joined up as a soldier but had

---

[1] John Clavell, *Recantation of an Ill-led Life*, 1634, p. 8.

spent all his money before the troops left. Then he would confess with heavy sighs how necessity had tempted him to rob. Whatever happened, he was sworn never to reveal the names of any of his accomplices.

The company obeyed always their chosen leader, and lay ambushed under his direction. Sunday was their favourite day, as the roads were quieter and the only travellers on them would be those with important luggage. They concealed their faces with masks and "chin-cloths," and, whenever necessary, disguised their voices by holding pebbles in their mouths. For the same purpose they kept in their lodgings "a variety of Periwigs," false beards, patches and plasters. The "certain Indicium" of a highwayman was the "incongruity of his bushy Beard and Face"; and bearded men were beginning to be regarded with some misgiving. The bundle at the traveller's saddle had to be caught with the left hand and the sword grasped in the right. The watchword was some innocent phrase like, "What's o'clock?" or "Ware's Post away," or "The Moone shines bright." A common trick in the Highway Law was for one of the gang to ride slowly along till he was overtaken by a group of travellers. He then approached the one who looked as if he were carrying the money and whispered confidentially in his ear that the other travellers were dangerous fellows and that this warning was an act of Christian charity. He then suggested that they should slacken pace and fall a brief way behind. The rest was easy.

The only danger came from the travellers who might be resolute men, or observant enough to note whether "the great bush beard and face agreed together." But even if the traveller had a pair of pistols (those "grim handfuls"), there was usually another member of the gang in ambush behind him. The inefficiency of the Watchmen, poore, silly, old, decrepid Men, was proverbial, a matter of mockery among the highwaymen. The great robber, John Clavell, remarks:

> I never past by, but the watchman gave
> Me courteous language, wishing me to have
> A speciall care I was not rob'd.[1]

The Hue and Cry was again and again called out after the men of the road, but was seldom effective. The highwayman knew every corner of his chosen beat, and would either lead the pursuit across the countryside or "squat like a hare" and let them pass.

They largely adopted the vocabulary of the beggars. When they rode to rob houses, they took with them the "Hobgoblin" or "Little Snakesman," a boy concealed in a cask. The "Ken-Miller" took the cask into the house and left it there like another Wooden Horse, so that the boy (once known as the Kinchin Cove) might open the doors to them. The highwayman was known as the "Scupper"; his victim as the "Martin."

But the life of a highwayman offered to the lone rider prizes more glittering than those that fell to the gang. A solitary thief was as formidable as twenty, if he shouted from behind his mask to imaginary confederates; and he could escape as easily.

---

[1] *Recantation of an Ill-led Life*, p. 37.

Throughout these declining years of the Beggars' Brotherhood isolated heroes of the roads continue to appear, romantic figures in lace and satin. If the more neurotic among them, like Jackson, "slumbered out the tedious minutes of the gloomy night in horror and affrightment," most were content enough with "spending high and faring deliciously," with cramming their brief hazardous lives full of splendour and excitement before they swung as moral object lessons on the gallows. The great highwayman dressed and acted as a fine gentleman, thereby putting suspicion off the scent. Crowder is said to have robbed in the disguise of a bishop, accompanied by four or five reverend attendants; and there were a hundred stories of their courtesy and courage.

They were usually of scholarly and dignified appearance, like the "genteel-looking man" who held up Partridge and Tom Jones near Barnet. These were known as "Royal Scamps," as opposed to the mere "Scamp" like Turpin. They upheld very jealously the etiquette of their profession. John Everett proudly claims to be able to "lay as fair a claim to these good qualities as ever anyone that followed the Calling," and of the same arrogant nature was the romantic and indomitable Claude Du Vall.

Everyone knows the exploits of this personable knave, and how he danced a masterly coranto in his riding boots; and there was the same air of gaiety and daring even in the shabbiest of his crimes. He seems to have gone to endless trouble to be picturesque, as when he robbed an old Beaconsfield farmer of a hundred pounds by dressing a dog up as the Devil and thus throwing the company into confusion. Though he was drunk when he was captured at the Hole-in-the-Wall in Chandos Street, his death was mourned by hundreds. The felon's body lay under a black pall in a chamber hung with funeral tapestry and crowded with wax tapers and melancholy mutes. It became the conventional thing for the highwayman who wished to reach the head of his profession to follow du Vall's example. Gallant John Everett used to rob on the highway in a red rug-coat with silver edgings, and apologized with charming diffidence for the shifts to which cruel necessity compelled him to stoop. When James Whitney was led to execution, he was followed along the road to the gallows by crowds of weeping ladies. "The Sun-shine of their prosperity lasts but a moment, not so long as to warm their hands by the blazing fire of their Prodigalitie, before cold Death comes and seizeth them."[1] But at least they were generous with their stolen money; and of all criminals the "Royal Scamps" were the most beloved.

The gangs varied in number. Often, like Turpin and King, they robbed in pairs. The gang of William Spiggot consisted of his friend Thomas Phillips, a clergyman, and an escaped lunatic named Burroughs, whose babblings brought them all three to the gallows. James Hind, however, headed a gang of forty or fifty men.

Captain Hind, the "Greatest Thief of his Age," was one of the earlier highwaymen and had been a friend of Moll Cutpurse. As a child, in the saddlery

---

[1] *Jackson's Recantation*, 1674, D3.

of Chipping Norton, he is supposed to have shown a passionate curiosity on the subject of crime; no uncommon trait in childhood, though "robbers generally begin by playing at Chuck, till by degrees they learn the art of Pilfering." But later, when he became apprenticed to a butcher, he showed a continual restlessness and discontent. In the reign of James the First a village was no place in which to pen a lad of mettle; and he managed to borrow forty shillings from his mother and set out for London. He must have ridden off, alone on the highway for the first time in his life, with splendid dreams of the riches of the great city, with no idea then in his mind of going on the Scamp and running the gauntlet of the gallows. Courage and ambition would set his feet on the ladder soon enough; but the forty shillings proved his immediate downfall. It was a tempting sum to a butcher's apprentice; and he wandered at nightfall into one of the famous taverns on the outskirts of London. The next morning he woke up in a prison with a headache and no penny left from his forty shillings.

This was the first step on his downward career. He had fallen in disgrace at the first onset, and had no means of getting home to Chipping Norton, even if he had wished. Moreover, he happened to be lying next to a drunken rascal named Allen, who most providentially offered to make Hind his servant. Hind accepted with delight, and one imagines him not disappointed to discover that Allen was the leader of a notorious gang of highwaymen on Shooter's Hill. He was duly initiated into the Brotherhood of the Blade, and, like Meriton

o

Latroon in a similar position, had to be blooded at once by a robbery. This was to be done on Shooter's Hill. The gang remained out of sight on their horses in the shadow of a little copse. Young Hind, when he saw the two travellers on the brow of the hill, rode out alone in the moonlight, brandishing his pistol. His voice did not tremble when he thundered the "Stand and deliver!" from behind his mask; nor did the frightened travellers guess that they handed their money-bags to a butcher-boy. When Hind rode back with his booty, Allen praised him for robbing "with a Grace."

Indeed, James Hind must have revealed his charm of manner very early. In the many exploits he performed with Allen's gang he showed such wit, such courtesy and daring, that he came to be spoken of in the neighbourhood as the leader. Allen grew jealous, and Hind chafed at having to share the booty he won among so many. He broke away from his companions and committed at last his first solo robbery. He came on an inn a little way from the road as dusk was falling; and, peering through the window, saw two travellers sitting drowsily before the fire. Near the door were their "Portmantles." Hind crept in, slit the boxes and was lucky enough to discover a large store of gold. He had scarcely got outside the door before one of the travellers awoke, saw the broken box, and gave the alarm. Hind, burdened by his plunder, was closely pursued. As he galloped down the road, he came upon a parson standing at the wayside; and, flinging himself from his horse, he caught him by the coat, exclaiming breathlessly: "Sir, I am like to be robbed, you must stand to it now for your own good as well as mine; they would have this money from me, which you see." The parson was obviously terrified; obviously beginning to say, "Nay, I am a man of peace——"

"Come, sir," cried Hind, hearing the thunder of those pursuing hoofs, "be of good cheer. One honest man will scare ten thieves; you shall have one of my pistols," and, thrusting the weapon into the hands of the trembling parson, he galloped away in the twilight. The parson fired as the pursuit thundered towards him, missed, hurled the pistol away and jumped into the ditch. He was bound and taken as a common thief before the justice. It was characteristic of Hind's humour and humanity to have chosen a churchman as his decoy. He knew that suspicion could not long have rested upon such a man. He must also have been fairly certain that none of the travellers would be injured by the parson's shot.

He shows the same relish for the incongruous or the ironical in many of his later deeds. He was fond of disguising himself as a theologically-minded shepherd, trudging along the roads, whistling lugubrious psalms and cracking unsuspecting wayfarers on the head with his crook. On one occasion he was himself held up by two highwaymen, but, charging full-tilt at them, he overthrew both from their horses. "There is but one master thief in England," he said, with genial contempt, to his crestfallen assailants, and flung back their purses. "Disgrace not yourselves with small sums," he told them, "but aim high for great ones; for the least will bring you to the gallows."[1]

---

[1] G. Fidge, *The English Gusman*, 1651, p. 4.

If his victim behaved well, Hind always returned the purse. He seems to have pursued his dangerous trade chiefly for the mere love of adventure. He took keen pleasure in wearing false beards and wigs, in adopting queer, incongruous disguises. He once dressed up as a woman, made love to a lawyer in the Devil Tavern and swindled him of a satisfactory sum. It was characteristic of him to waylay at the foot of Shotover Hill the wagon that contained the wages of the royal army, merely for the satisfaction of "fleecing those great thieves of Westminster." He seemed to lead an enchanted life; and was said to have had a magic compass given to him by a witch in Hatfield. It pointed always to the road where safety lay. He was never actually captured at his crimes, though Thomas Knowls, called "Hind's elder Brother," is supposed to have overcome him on one occaison—

> Thus Hind which knew the cutting Trade so well,
> Was robb'd by Knowls who did him farre excell
> In th' highway arts and in the padding skill,
> For Hind's in Newgate, and Knowls at freedome still.[1]

But Knowls's career was brief, and was to end also at Newgate; and before he came to that inevitable close and crown of his career, Hind was to make reputations in Holland, Scotland and the Isle of Man. England had become too hot to hold him; and it was rash to return to London in 1652. On November 9th information was given that this arch-robber was living under the name of Brown at a barber's in Fleet Street. He was captured and taken

---

[1] *The Master Thief Discovered*, 1652, p. 7.

to the condemned cell in Newgate. "Well," said he,
"All this I vallew not three pence. I owe a debt to
God, and a debt I must pay"; and in such a spirit
he stepped from the Tyburn ladder.

> *Hynd* of *Latrons* Lord and Chiefe;
> *Hynd*, the strong, but courteous Thiefe:
> He with whom *Clavell*, *Cheyny*, or
> *Luke Huttons* selfe might not compare,
> Heere lyes buried: Let him lye,
> Travailer, thou mayst passe by
> Safely now, maugre his view,
> With thy Purse and Money too.[1]

Hind's reputation was soon overshadowed by a
not less picturesque figure.

How vain are the thoughts of such, who whilst youth
and strength accompany them, never consider they are a
meer Statue of dust kneaded with Tears, and moved by
the hid engines of restless passions . . . instead thereof
they bounce so high, and make so much noise in the world,
as if both the globes (those glorious Twins) had been un-
wombed from the formless Chaos by the midwifery of
their brain.[2]

Such were the meditations of Jackson the Highwayman as he lay in the condemned cell at Newgate,
looking back over the marvellous villainies of his
career. He was melancholy enough, for it had all
come to an end now, and there would be no more
meetings in the tavern or reconciliations with his
beloved Mistresse, or rides in the moonlight over
Marlborough Downs. And yet, searching over all
those adventurous years, he had bounced high

---

[1] *Last Will & Testament of James Hynd*, 1651, p. 6.
[2] *Jackson's Recantation*, 1674, A1.

enough and made noise enough in the world; and there was some small consolation in thinking of the humble ragged creature he had once been.

His life had begun in poverty and unhappiness; and he could trace the whole subsequent history of his crimes from the lucky finding of a wallet in the road. He had stumbled upon it by chance, and found it full of guineas, and what desperate gutter-urchin would not have used this to buy new clothes and travel to London? It had been well enough if it had stopped there. But, setting up as the son of a country gentleman, he had fallen in with a company of Coney-catchers, "incomparable in the art of Wheedling," and it was not long before he became apprentice to a master card-sharper. Jackson remained all his life the shrewd fearless gamin he had been among the Coney-catchers of the London streets. He became indispensable to the gang as a decoy, and spent his time hunting for rich simpletons among the theatres, cock-pits and Ordinaries. He and his master studied together the art of winning the confidence of conies. They would, after the imme-morial traditions of their trade, strike up acquaintance with some young leisured gull, offer to lend him money or to befriend him among the subtle tempta-tions of the London streets. Or they would pretend that some old enemy was eager to pick a quarrel. Jackson would offer to fight for the coney, and appear the next morning woefully bandaged. The coney, of course, paid for a non-existent doctor, and might even be grateful enough to put down a substantial sum in recompense for his deliverer. And "when all his money is spent, his Credit gone and destroyed, and his Father hearing of his son's extravagancies, and what desolate, desperate company he keeps, then we think it is time to vanish."[1]

The game could not last. The Coney-catcher's was a hazardous business, and it was becoming less and less easy to find young men who had never read the pamphlets of Greene and Rowlands. Coney-catchers were more numerous than conies, and when Jackson's tutor and companion died, he was in pitiful case. One day, walking moodily in Hatton Gardens, he met with a gang of four Knights of the Road, who led him jovially to a tavern. He was not long in making up his mind. He swore the oaths of the Brotherhood, purchased a horse and rode with them out of town.

They dined in Maidenhead that night, and travelled on after sunset along the road to Reading, "making a little halt by the way at Maidenhead Thicket." One of the inns they patronized stood a little way back from the road, and from the landlord who "winkt at them" they learnt of a gentleman who was on the way to Marlborough with a promisingly large Portmantue. Jackson, whose long practice had made him the most affable of companions, fell into conversation with the traveller, and was obligingly warned by him of a "parcel of Whipper-Snappers" who rode on Marlborough Downs. They sat up late, heartening each other against the dangers of the roads. The traveller at length became confidential and showed Jackson his ingenious method of concealing treasure under his saddle. The rest, for the parcel of Whipper-Snappers who waited in the

[1] *Jackson's Recantation*, B3v.

thicket outside, was easy; though Jackson received
a well-deserved bullet in the arm.

It was not always so easy. They once robbed
a number of seamen near Chatham, taking over
£180. One of the seamen showed great eagerness
to join the Brotherhood, and after some discussion
was sworn and admitted. He and Jackson rode
along together talking amicably of their plans and
the plunder they hoped to win. "At length," says
Jackson, "riding in a Lane, suspecting nothing in
the least, he turns his little Hobby upon me, and
seizing my Bridle before I was aware, claps to my
Breast a little ugly Brass-barrelled Pistol and swore
as bloodily as if he had been one of the Trade above
twenty years, if I would not instantly dismount,
he would send a Bullet to my heart." He was lucky
to have escaped so easily. Indeed, pondering in the
underground cell on his adventures, he marvels that
he bore so long a charmed life. It was like a run
of luck in a gambling den; but, however long the
cards held, luck turned in the end. The Brotherhood
were taken ignominiously on the road. The game
was over and the score paid on the gallows. Jackson
hung in chains at Hampstead, "a sad and dreadful
Spectacle to all Beholders."

It is not very easy to see how such a character
became a hero of legends among the country folk.
It is harder still to understand how his famous successor, Richard Turpin, won his romantic position—
a position established long before *Rookwood* gave him
his undeserved reputation for gallantry. The tales
of Black Bess and the ride to York are as fantastically
false as the tales of the treasure of Captain Kidd.

Turpin was a brutal, ill-educated ruffian whose murders were mean and whose thefts had nothing of the audacity and imagination that redeemed the actions of Captain Hind. Like Hind, he was apprenticed to a butcher, but appeared to enjoy this method of expressing his crude, sadistic tendencies. When for crooked dealing he was compelled to go out of business, he fell in with a gang of deer-stealers in Epping Forest and began his career as a house-breaker. The tales of his thefts are numerous and un-pleasant. He once put an old lady to roast on her own fire in order to compel her to reveal where she had hidden her money. He was merely the most brutal of a gang of brutal ruffians, systematically attacking house after house along the less crowded byways. They used to tie the inmates hand and foot, threatening to murder them if they made a sound; and then, after stripping the house, would sit together in the kitchen eating and drinking all they had been able to discover in the larder.

The gang did not last long; and Turpin took to the roads on his own. Riding one day along the Cambridge road, he met a "stout man in a white duffil coat" and mounted on a magnificent horse. Turpin presented his pistol and demanded exchange of mounts. He was greeted with a peal of laughter. "What! Dog eat dog?" cried the stranger. "Come, come, brother Turpin, if you don't know me, I know you, and shall be glad of your company"—and he revealed himself as the highwayman, King. The two formed a partnership which did no good to King, for Turpin was a sorry companion even for a thief. They shared together their headquarters, a cave near Epping Forest, where they could sit and watch the travellers passing on the road below. They began collaborating in a series of sordid and tedious crimes. Turpin lacked imagination, and seems to have pursued his dingy calling by some animal instinct, some in-bred savagery in his nature. He shot a man named Thompson who chanced to find the cave; and was thereafter forced to abandon these quarters, taking to the roads and sleeping where he could, a felon with a big price on his head.

It was not long before King was taken; and Turpin, in attempting to release him, shot him by mistake. He now became like some wild, stupid animal, skulking alone in the thickets of Epping till even that fastness could not longer conceal him. He fled to Yorkshire under the name of John Palmer, and was almost at once arrested and flung into gaol. He seems to have become human only at the very end of his life. He bought a new fustian frock and a pair of pumps for his execution, and carefully hired five poor men of the town to mourn for him. On the way to the gallows he bowed right and left to the spectators like royalty in a procession. His body was torn out of its deep grave by the Resurrection Men. . . .

It was a sordid finish to a thwarted and desperate life. But, whether it was the fustian coat, or whether it was the mere appalling number of the crimes he committed, ever since the day of his execution, Turpin's name conjured up an accumulation of mysterious and romantic legends.

One of the very last of the highwaymen was the curious and eccentric James Aitkin, known also as

James Hill, Jack Hind and Jack the Painter. In his queer autobiography he tells how, business being bad, he bought a pair of pistols and "proceeded to Finchley Common," where he successfully robbed a number of post-chaises. For some years he kept himself in comfort with a series of road and street robberies, but a strange obsession altered his method of life.

One night, being in conversation concerning the American War, the importance of His Majesty's fleet and dockyards was the favourite argument; and it was with satisfaction that I heard everyone agree that the safety, the welfare and even the existence of this nation depended on them.

This conversation haunted him, till he came to be convinced that it would be a heroic action to destroy the docks, and that if he succeeded in doing so he would be acclaimed as the saviour and deliverer of America. Accordingly he arrived in Portsmouth one Thursday evening, burdened with parcels of gunpowder and turpentine. He made careful preparations and succeeded in setting light to his various trains, though he found himself locked by some unsuspecting workman in the hemp-house, and actually had to knock on the wall and call to be let out. His disappointment was great when he discovered on the following morning that none of his machines had taken effect. He failed again at Plymouth, and, in a rage, decided to destroy Bristol entirely, town and shipping. In a dozen Bristol warehouses he laid trains of matches; and this time came near to success.

Turning round I thought the whole element was in flames, so dreadful was the appearance it had at that distance, which tempted me to return to be an eye-witness of the destruction I had wrought. On my near approach the flames seemed to abate; but I found the whole city in consternation and terror; though my schemes had not answered my full intentions. My matches had only taken effect in Quay Lane among the warehouses of Mr. Brown the bookseller . . .

In despair, he turned for a few days to his old trade of robbery; but his hand seemed to have lost its cunning. He was captured, confessed with a kind of quiet pride the failure of his attempt to deliver the Americans, and hung in tarry chains from the mizen-mast of the *Arethusa* for many years, a grim and pitiable sight.

So, like their forerunners who canted at the road's edge, the company of the highwaymen dwindled in a losing fight against the law. But during their century and a half of power, they aroused more terror and won more admiration than ever had fallen to the lot of the Beggars' Brotherhood. The very things—the lace ruffles, the pistols, the masked malignant face—that had been the cause of so much fear, became finally the trappings of romance. Where the wooden bowl of the beggar was forgotten, the challenge of the highwayman and the story of his deeds were remembered long after the last of the hooves had gone thundering down the moonlit roads.

DICK SWIFT.

Thieftaker, Teaching his Son the Commandments.

XIV

THE LAST OF THE CONEY-CATCHERS

So the Brotherhood of Beggars, after its brief prosperity, declined, gave birth to the Highwaymen, and perished. And so also the great gangs of the Coney-catchers became transformed beyond recognition. The old rush to wealth and London, the spacious days, had passed for good; folk were growing more sober, more cautious, more law-abiding. The Bow Street Runners were beginning to oust the inefficient and decrepit Watch; and Henry Fielding had laid the foundations of the modern police force. "I undertook," he writes on his last voyage, "to demolish the then reigning gangs, and to put the civil policy into such order, that no such gangs should ever be able, for the future, to form themselves into bodies, or at least to remain any time formidable to the public."

It was a death-knell. The Coney-catcher became rarer. He could no longer join in bands with his fellows, but lurked, dangerous and solitary, on the outskirts of society. Gradually he became not a menace but a despised and miserable parasite; nearer and nearer the glib, ingratiating man one meets in third-class railway carriages with a green cloth over his knees and a handful of greasy cards. Indeed, it was at this time that the earliest form of the three-card trick made its appearance. It was done with three thimbles and a button, and known as the Thimble Rig.

The Thimble player in Appearance is very regardless
how much he exposes the Button to the View of the Countryman, but in reality, shifts it by a Trick of Dexterity betwixt
his fingers under another Thimble; so that the poor Fellow
having so lost his money, the Accomplice takes up the right
Thimble, and blames the Countryman for his mistake.[1]

The Coney-catcher did not entirely disappear.
In a structure so wide and loose as that of modern
society there are enough shabby corners for him
to hide in. But he no longer showed his face openly
in the taverns nor cheated a royal way to the gallows.
The *Beggar's Opera* was the sufficient epitaph for
the gangs of tramps and crooks the terror of whose
name had once overshadowed the entire country.
It reveals the gallants of George II's court laughing
at that band which had been the scourge of their
ancestors. Macheath is a merry, singing shadow;
too idealized even to be dirty. Their jests are no
longer the grim taunts of men who never anticipated
the dawn and who knew they might, any morning,
suffer the fate of their "glad, mad brother" of the
fifteenth century—

> Qui, d'une corde d'une toise,
> Scaura mon col que mon cul poise.

The beggar and the Coney-catcher henceforth became
romantic only in the pages of picturesque novels.

"Know ye, therefore," says Mary Frith, "O all ye
Pickpockets, Lifters, Heavers, Rumpads, Bawds etc.
that . . . we have prosecuted the discovery of all
the Arts and Artifices, for which your Governesse
was famous. . . . Read therefore if you can spare

---

[1] *The Thief-Catcher*, 1753, p. 15.

time from your Businesse, the sad decayes of your
Trade."

Sad decayes, indeed. Throughout the seventeenth
century the Coney-catchers were losing ground, becoming less and less of an organization, more and
more mere scattered bands of knaves. These at
times aimed high enough. One of them was led
by Thomas Sadler, hanged eventually at Tyburn.
They stole the mace and purse of Lord Chancellor
Finch, and held a midnight procession, bearing
their trophies shoulder-high through the streets.
They then concealed the spoil in their lodgings,
but the daughter of the house, as daughters of the
house will, peered through the keyhole and ran
downstairs, gleefully crying, "Mother, mother!
Yonder is the King's Crown in our Closet!"

A similar crime was committed by the notorious
Colonel Blood, "villain complete in parson's gown,"
who stole the Crown and Sceptre from the Tower
in 1670. This was one of the boldest and most ingeniously planned robberies of the century. It was
an elaborate and Raffles-like piece of strategy.
The Colonel, who had, like so many of his kind,
a genius for disguise, dressed up as a parson and
visited the Tower, bringing with him a wench who
pretended to be his wife. The "wife" fell into a
realistic swoon in the chamber where the crown
jewels were kept. Talbot Edwards, the Keeper of
the Regalia, offered her stimulants and she was
entertained by Mrs. Edwards till she had at length
recovered.

This casual meeting began an acquaintance
sedulously fostered by Colonel Blood, till it ripened

to such an extent that a few weeks later he could propose a marriage between his nephew and Edwards's daughter. On the day appointed for the marriage, Blood arrived at the Tower with two men, both attired in the height of fashion, as befitted a bridegroom and a best man, and wearing extravagantly wide breeches. They had come rather early, and the bride was not yet ready. They suggested they might pass the time by looking at the Crown jewels. No sooner had they entered the room than they attacked the unfortunate Edwards, gagged him with a wooden wedge and even passed an iron hook through his nose to prevent him from uttering the smallest sound. Finally they also stabbed him, to make quite sure, and left him as they thought dead on the floor. One of the conspirators hid the orb in his voluminous trousers and under his wide parson's cloak Blood concealed the crown. But Edwards was not dead, and his daughter happened to come into the room only a few seconds after Blood had left. The thieves were caught with the jewels still on them.

The adventure had a curious sequel. Charles II interviewed Blood and was so well impressed by his personality that he refused to punish him, and even returned to him the Irish estates which had long before been forfeited.

But such ambitious rogues lived a century too late. Their fellow-thieves were of a meaner sort. The eighteenth century seems to us a century of meanness and gloom and squalor. Far more sordid appear the dram-shops and the cut-throats in those dusky alleys than the violent robbers of the Elizabethan age. Gin was the triumphant spirit of the century and even in Fielding's day, the gangs, though no longer organized in a Brotherhood, were as savage and formidable as they had ever been. The "Mob" was a real menace; though we use the word loosely enough to-day to describe any gathering of people we consider inferior to ourselves. Two hundred years ago it meant a clan of Whitefriars desperadoes, ever on the verge of breaking forth, like some depraved and furious animal, to shatter windows and burn houses and riot along the twilit streets.

But a real and gradually successful warfare was begun by the Court Justice, Colonel de Veil, in the early years of the century; and if one could choose any date to mark the end of the brotherhoods of thieves, one would choose 1750, the year of the first tentative move towards a State Police force. It was in that year that Henry Fielding had under him a troop of some eighty constables, the earliest paid police force in the country. Fielding swore to finish once and for all the reign of the brotherhood of thieves, one gang of which he says "falls little short of a hundred, who are incorporated in one body, have officers and a treasury; and have reduced theft and robbery to a regular system."

There were several of these scattered troops in London, living, like Colonel Jack, under the arches of bridges and sleeping on doorsteps. Jack himself became apprenticed in the usual way to an expert Foist, and they attended Bartholomew Fair and prowled about Bednall Green or the huddle of slum roofs on the Bankside in the shadow of St. Mary

P

Overy. The old watchwords, "Good Tower Standard," and "Mark, ho!" were still used, but the old meeting-places were being built over or had become too well known to the authorities. The ale of the tavern had yielded to the "soot-coloured ninny-broth" of the coffee-houses. The haunts of the Coney-catchers became for a time the "Chapter" of Paternoster Row, where the grave booksellers used to gather, the "Rainbow" in Fleet Street or "Tom's" of Birchin Lane. By Jonathan Wild's day they had given place to the gin-shops, where "after having drunk plente-ously of Spirituous Liquors so as to have primed their Evil Genius's for the most desperate Scenes of Villainy, they divide into Troops and Squadrons to range the whole City and Avenues thereof, where, they knock down, cut, wound, and sometimes murder and always rob what people they meet alone in the streets."

Somehow they seem to lack the stature of their forerunners; or it may be merely that they lived in a less wildly romantic age and had less opportunity for knavery. Major Clancie, a contemporary of Bampfylde-Moore Carew and Meriton Latroon, was typical of the seventeenth-century Coney-catcher. He fell into thievery picturesquely, for, happening to try on some of his master's clothes and seeing the effect in a mirror, he was so impressed that he could not resist running off to London with the entire wardrobe.

This was the first step on that career which gave him later the wholly undeserved title of "Grandest Cheat of his Age." He posed as one of the witty, accomplished crooks, for ever at a "pretty pitch of

Jolitry," but his cheats were sordid affairs, unredeemed by a shadow of jolitry. He was continually repenting and turning over new leaves; and on one occasion went so far as to become a Franciscan monk. Brother Clancie ran off with the monastery cash, and returned to his old trade. Nell's Ordinary was his familiar haunt. The big, red-faced, weak-mouthed man was very friendly to any strangers who happened to come in for a drink. He became an accomplished Courtesy Man, and must have had a winning personality, for he made himself so agreeable to one chance visitor at the Ordinary that they both clasped hands and swore to regard each other as bloodbrothers. It was not long before Major Clancie took advantage of his new-found relationship to remark, "Brother, if I am not mistaken, I heard you wish for a friend that would be true to you, and could help you to your money upon your arrival in Paris." In return for a forged i o u on a mythical Earl, he persuaded his "brother" to advance him £200.

This trick landed the Major in Newgate, where "with some success" he made love to the Marshal's only daughter, and with her assistance actually persuaded the Marshal to set him free—only to return once more on a still drearier charge. He could never alter his nature. As a young man he had been so gay and genial a companion that men forgave him much. As he grew older he grew a little fat; a little coarse and self-indulgent. Every face can be a diary of old debauches after a certain age; and Clancie's life had left its marks. He became an outcast, shunned by his betrayed and cheated friends. His tricks grew more and more dismal, more and more shabbily futile; because the ladder of crime hangs down over an abyss, and each step he took landed him a little lower, till he stepped into nothing from the tail of Tyburn cart.

The Coney-catchers of the eighteenth century had their "shifts" like the Elizabethans; but very few of the old Laws had survived. The Courtesy Man was succeeded by the Cadator, in about 1690. The Cadator was a travelling Mr. Sponge, who made an exhaustive study of the genealogies of great families, and journeyed round England gaining hospitality from each of them in turn. The counterfeit dicers still plied their trade under the name of Tattogeys, but they were found no longer at fashionable Ordinaries or coffee-houses. They had already sunk to haunting country fairs and markets.

Cheaters' Gambling dens still obscurely flourished, but gambling was becoming more and more the sport of the middle classes, and the Coney-catchers found their conies more adept than themselves. There were mysterious "machines called Rowlipolly"; and there was a special Law known as "Sweetners," invented solely for the purpose of deceiving parsons. There was an incredible number of Orange Dicers about the town. These were men who wheeled round the streets barrows piled with oranges, and who were followed at a discreet distance by a confederate. The confederate came up to the Orange seller in some crowded place and offered to throw dice, with the fruit as a stake. A crowd gathered; the orange seller lost all his fruit and recklessly offered then to gamble with money. Some coney would be certainly deceived and, thinking the man a ninny, ventured his money, which would eventually be sufficient to buy a new load of oranges and leave a handsome margin of profit.

John Poulter, who headed a Coney-catching gang in the early eighteenth century, made a curious list of the "Laws." The Lifting Law was practised in his day by women who secreted goods from shop-windows under innumerable petticoats. The Nip cut purses as of old, but referred to his business now as "the great Trade or knowing Art called *Filing*." The Ring Faller practised the Fawney Rig or the Art of Old Nobbs. The rest of them had disappeared; or had become changed beyond report, thought or belief.

But new and ingenious methods of cosenage had been invented. The Art of Ringing Tuggs was sublimely simple.

People in Fairs or Markets in the Summer are apt to give their greatcoats to the Maid, and put their names on it with a piece of paper. The servant cannot remember every coat, and the Sharper comes in and writes his Name on his Coat that is worth but little and changes his Note to another Coat.[1]

There is a surprisingly modern ring in this device as also in a delightful Coney-catching device peculiar to barbers. A chatty barber would inform his customer that he needed a new ribbon for his queue, and promise to get him one for a shilling. The barber then bought a ribbon for eightpence, hastily ironed out the old ribbon and slipped it on again, ingeniously ringing the changes for several weeks on the two ribbons,

[1] *Discoveries of John Poulter*, 1751, p. 35.

till the customer had given him a reasonable margin of profit. There was also the trick of insinuating lice into the hair and thereby inducing clients to undergo expensive treatments.

Numberless small fry roamed the town. There were the Tickers who existed by an elaborate system of buying goods on "tick," dodging like Dick Swiveller from shop to shop. The Morning Sneak, descendant of the Budge, hung around the streets after the breakfast hour, waiting for the householder to set out on his business and give him an opportunity of nipping inside. Cat-burgling, "Kinning by the Parapet," was done by the Jacobs who went "with Ladders in the Dead of the Night," climbed to the tops of the houses and scrambled from roof to roof till they chanced on an open attic window.

There were gangs of these burglars. Jack Hall, the Chimney Sweep who as a boy had been ducked in the village horse pond, whipped at Bridewell and branded on the cheek, formed a gang with Richard Low and Stephen Bounce. They terrorized the town for a brief period by a number of senselessly savage thefts; they often threatened to roast their victims in ovens to make them reveal where they hid their money, and on once occasion tied up the family of a baker and threw them all together into the kneading trough. They scattered after a time and disappeared. Jack Hall represented them on the gallows.

> Where art thou now, thou Reprobate,
> Who jested'st at a future state?[1]

---

[1] *Rogues Calendar, Elegy on Jack Hall*, 1784.

There were crowds of nameless bullies who made a speciality of attacking midnight revellers returning from the houses of the great. "It is the general Complaint," says the *Regulator* in 1718, "of the Taverns, the Coffee Houses, the Shopkeepers and others, that many of their Customers are afraid when it is dark, to come to their Houses and shops, for fear that their Hats and Wigs should be snatched from off their Heads, or their Swords taken from their Sides, or that they may be blinded, knocked down, cut or stabbed." There was little difference between these mobs of thieves and the Sons of Belial, flown with insolence and wine, who slit noses as a form of self-expression. Most of the later Coney-catchers practised more harmless devices. One, the "Rum-Snooser," attached pieces of paper to the hats of topers as they lay sleeping off the effects of their potations at the tavern window. He then set the paper alight and when the victim awoke he found his wig burnt. For the complete success of the trick the victim had to leap from his seat offering rewards if anyone would tell him the author of the outrage. "It was a coachman who has run upstairs," the Rum-Snooser would reply, and as the coney thundered in pursuit the Rum-Snooser would nip down the street with anything he could lay hands on. Another, called the "Queer Plunger," imposed on the Royal Humane Society of the day. Queer Plungers worked in gangs of three. One would fall into the river; another heroically rescue him and the third restore him to life. They would then collect money from the crowd for the unfortunate man and apply even for medals to decorate his rescuer.

The wrecks on the Cornish coasts and the enormous strides taken in surgery and physiology were responsible for stratagems more sinister. In Cornwall the crime called by the grotesque name of Jibber the Kibber appeared frequently throughout the eighteenth century. Wreckers hung a lantern on a horse's head and bound one of the animal's legs up so that it limped. They led it along the cliffs in the hope than on dark nights ships at sea would mistake it for the bow-light of another vessel. So the miserable mariners were deceived and came "bounce ashore in an instant."

The Resurrection Rig was also an eighteenth-century development; and because the interests of science gave it a certain excuse, was carried on in open defiance of the law. Even in the sixteenth century the "barber-surgeons" had customarily been given a few bodies of the hanged to anatomize. Resurrection Men made a practice of stealing corpses from graveyards and selling them to surgeons for what they could get.

> When they hear a passing bell toll, they skulk about the parish from ale-house to ale-house, till they can learn a proper account of what the deceased died of, what condition the body is in, etc.[1]

At midnight they dug the corpse up and warehoused it. Twenty dead bodies were once discovered stored in a shed in Tottenham Court Road; and they were moved one by one to the mortuary by hackney coachmen with large hampers. The bodies of Laurence Sterne and Jonathan Wild were disturbed in this

[1] G. Parker, *View of Society and Manners*, 1781, II, 145.

way, and several famous surgeons like John Hunter were known to be regularly supplied by the Resurrection Men. Only legislation by Parliament in the nineteenth century finally stopped the trade.

There were rogues about in hundreds, but acting for the most part on their own. The *Regulator* gives a list, like Harman's, of notable London thieves. There was Blue Sue, Dancing Doll's incredible daughter; and Sarah Hull, "who has had three Husbands hanged and the fourth condemned four times." There was that expert Nip, Little Arthur Chambers, the "Prince of Prigs." The flash gaming houses were their principal nurseries; and it was from one of these that the portent known as Jenny Diver appeared.

Her real name was Mary Young. For some time she lived at Long Acre with a woman called Ann Murphy, and was introduced by her to a kind of Pickpockets' Club near St. Giles. It was not long before Mary Young's skill in pickpocketing earned her her nickname; and she became acknowledged Queen of the Foists. She distinguished herself by making a pair of wooden hands and sitting in church with them demurely folded in her lap, while she was free to snatch what she could from her neighbours. At length she became rich enough to have a personal footman of her own, and to live in pomp at Covent Garden, where she practised Coney-catching in a more subtle way. Twice her adventures landed her in Newgate; twice she was transported, and finally, unrepentant to the last, was hanged at Tyburn.

There was only one Jenny Diver. The cheats exposed by Tom Brown and a host of eighteenth-century chap-books are no longer the cheats of a brotherhood but the ingenuities of individuals. A little tract on the *Art of Living in London* commenting on the gangs who "live only by cheating," notes their sad decline as early as 1642. "If you are a countryman," says the author, "and but newly come to town, you will be smelt out by some cheaters or other, who will salute you, call you by your name . . . and carry you to a tavern." But he adds, "all tricks of late years have been so plainly discovered and are so generally known almost to every child, that their practice is out of date, and now no great fear of them."

There was, however, in the early years of the eighteenth century, a sudden, terrifying recrudescence of the brotherhood of thieves under the leadership of one man. Defoe estimated that at one time Jonathan Wild controlled an organization of more than seven thousand thieves. He was one of the earliest of the Thief-takers, an abuse which began late in the seventeenth century. The idea was that the Thief-taker should be a kind of spy on behalf of the Government, that he should insinuate himself into the confidence of the thieves and betray them one by one to the gallows, building the foundations of their trade on the old proverb, "Old Theeves make good Gaolers." Actually he would run with the hare and hunt with the hounds. While taking the Government's rewards for betraying the criminals, he would also take bribes from the criminals themselves, claiming a large share in their profits. He would even plan and arrange robberies in order to get shares in the reward offered by the Government and hush-money from the thieves. It worked well. The Thief-taker became intimate with three of the more notorious robbers in the early part of the century—William and Christopher Matthews and Obadiah Lemmon. The three thieves stole a purse from a lady; the lady applied to the Thief-taker, who denounced anyone against whom he happened to have a grudge. The two "Shim-sham thieves" were safely imprisoned, and Christopher, William, Obadiah and the Thief-taker shared the reward.

Dick Swift was a notorious and highly successful Thief-taker, and his tavern, the "Dun House," was a favourite meeting-place for thieves. It became customary for travellers to call at the "Dun House" and inquire the password which would allow them to pass along the roads unhindered by Swift's gangs. A pleasant old print shows him teaching his son the Ten Commandments—his thumb tactfully concealing the "not" in the eighth. The promising lad is paying grave attention to his father's words while taking the opportunity at the same time of picking his pocket.

The professional Receiver appeared when the Government had made it a felony to harbour stolen goods. The innkeepers and pawnbrokers gave smaller and smaller sums for the spoil that came into their hands; and the Thief-taker, acting in a semi-official position, could afford to bid higher, carrying on the illicit trade of Receiver under the shadow of his business as a Thief-taker.

Chance turned Wild into the greatest criminal organizer of his day. He was imprisoned for four years in the Wood Street Compter, and it was there that he made acquaintance with most of the thieves in London. Those vile monsters danced attendance on their ringmaster for twenty years. Joseph Blake was there, known as Blueskin from his swarthy face, William Field, Lindsay the eccentric and degenerate clergyman who rode the highway with Spiggot and Phillips, James Sykes (familiarly known as "Hell and Fury"), and poor depraved indomitable Sheppard. There too was the infamous Mary Milliner, whose ear Wild once cut off in a fit of fury and who was the first person with whom he became intimate.

The two bought a tavern together in Cock Alley, opposite Cripplegate Church; and it was here that Wild set up as a Fence or Receiver. Knowing the face and record of every notable knave in London, he formed what Borrow called "a corporation of thieves," and appointed gangs to work for him in various districts throughout the city. At the height of his power he had London at his feet. The under-world found in him its first and last Napoleon. He could exercise a general blackmail, and if any member of his gangs proved refractory, he would say, mean-ingly, "I have given you my word that you should come and go in safety, and so you shall; but take care of yourself; for if ever you see me again, you see an enemy."

He was not without his rivals. Chief among these was Charles Hitchin, ex-City Marshal, who patrolled the streets capturing thieves and threatening to denounce them unless he were given a share of their takings. After a brief truce, Wild and Hitchin openly quarrelled, attacking each other in a series of violent pamphlets. Chief among these was Hitchin's *Regulator:*

a Discovery of Theeves and Thief Takers, in which "his skittish and Baboonish Majesty" Jonathan Wild was scurrilously attacked. But they were both too sensible not to realize how much greater would be their profits if they amalgamated; and about 1720 they controlled between them every gang of thieves throughout the city. They were acknowledged overlords of the Southwark Mint. At a moment's notice they could lay their hands on any thief in London.

Wild's escapes were miraculous. When he himself was laid at last by the heels, his body was found to be covered from head to foot with old scars. Blueskin, the pickpocket, having been assiduously ushered to the gallows, attempted to slit Wild's throat with a penknife, unhappily blunt. His failure was a heavy blow, and he took to drinking heavily, being hanged in a state of profound intoxication.

The office of Thief-taker really became a kind of school or forcing house for crime, and the Thief-taker himself a schoolmaster in the art of robbery.

Question. What are all that heap of Boys at that Table, that are playing at Dice, swearing, cursing, and grinning at each other, like so many Hell-cats; and that Man in the silver-button'd Coat and Knotted Peruke . . .?
Answer. Sir, those boys are all . . . Pickpockets, and that Man in the silver-button'd Coat is their Thief-Taker . . . and I suppose he is now asking them, if they have any such for him at present, or putting them in mind, that he expects to be served by them for the future.[1]

Wild himself made an art of roguery. It was fitting that no less a man than Henry Fielding, J.P., should

[1] *Regulator*, p. 12.

have written the epic of the last of the Coney-catchers, and his magnificently ironic portrait is probably not very much overdrawn. "A bold heart, a thundering voice, and a steady countenance" he numbers among Wild's "more transcendental qualities." Among others, Wild's maxims were never to do unnecessary mischief, "for mischief is too precious a thing to be thrown away"; to sacrifice all to self-interest; never forgive, but be cold and lingering in vengeance; to encourage jealousy between members of one's gang; never to hesitate in risking one's good name, and to shun any kind of poverty or unhappiness. He lived recklessly, bullying a crowd of rogues and murderers with his loud harsh voice. But this little irritable man with the scornful mouth did not die as he should. He lost his nerve, and in a strange terror asked on the day he was executed, the meaning of the words, "Cursed is everyone that hangeth on a tree." He took a dose of laudanum and swung, half-drowsed, at Tyburn amid the appalling execrations of the mob. It would have been more in character with his life if he had gaily scorned the gallows, crying, "Damme, it is only a dance without music!" or if he had picked the Ordinary's pocket of a corkscrew to equip himself for the first toast he drank in hell.

But "I will stirre this Puddle no longer, nor dive into the depth of it any further, least I pollute and inquinate the Reader." With the end of Wild and the disbanding of the gangs he had for so long controlled, came the final breakdown of the Brotherhood. Never again was there any unity among the criminals against the law. The saying "as thick as thieves" lost half the meaning it had had in the days when thieves really were thick; and the place of the early organization of beggars and cheats was taken by sinister and formidable outlaws, working on their own, or by the great financial brigands of a more civilized world.

ENDING

THE old order passed, yielding place to new. The life of the tramp is no longer a romantic adventure in the eyes of W. H. Davies, but a sordid procession from one brick workhouse to another. Even the gypsies grew ashamed of the title they were once proud enough to bear—

"You are one of them," said I, "whom people call——"
"Just so," said Jaspar, "but never mind what people call us."

For we live in a sadder and more sober world, where men no longer keep sheep out there on moonlit heaths. Sometimes, coming upon a bent and withered rascal at the pavement's edge, one has a sudden vision of those thousands of truculent mumpers, of whom he is the sole survivor. It is as if one had turned over a page in history, or found in some old lady's suburban drawing-room the parrot that was companion to Long John Silver and had seen Flint die shouting for rum. For, in a better-constituted world, if there is still room for Coney-catching, there is less and less room for the beggar. It is a comforting thought; though I should have enjoyed a meeting with that Upright Man to whom Dorothy Wordsworth once gave a piece of cold bacon and a penny. ("You're a fine woman!" he said.) In the old sense of the word, tramps are becoming an extinct race. A day will come when one will be ashamed to be seen on foot; one will take walks furtively, or at least with the same dim sense of shame with which

Q

one enters a pawnbroker's or a pub, a thing not
to be seen doing too often. And grim-faced men will
roar along the roads, stabbing iron pedals with their
feet. And perhaps in the end the human leg will
become as vestigial as the appendix or the pineal
eye, a paralysed and pendulous futility to remind
one of the queer pursuits of one's ancestors.

So the whole story of the beggars, their ragged
rise to power, their long warfare with sanity and
sanitation, their gradual decline, has become a
dusty and remote page in history. The tramp, the
Coney-catcher, the highwayman are remembered
now only as trappings to forgotten times, like warming-
pans and blunderbusses. " 'Tis ill," as Bunyan
would say, "pudling in the Cocatrice's den"; and
the Clapperdudgeon and the Hectoring Blade are
as remote now and fantastic as that polluting
beast.

You may ask where this once magnificent Brotherhood is gone; into what secret fastnesses of sin has
been driven the old fraternity of the Coney-catchers.
Perhaps even to-day you might meet the last survivor
on some deserted heath under the sky, shaving by
a broken mirror in a striped caravan. You may
meet him telling fortunes or picking pockets at a
country fair. Or you may meet him, as I did, one
winter twilight in the melancholy wastes of Tottenham
Court Road.

He was in rags, snuffling miserably into a tattered
handkerchief. He looked at me bleakly for a moment
with his blear solitary eye, and suddenly holding
out his hand, he muttered:

"Matches, sir?"

I thought of the last speech of Ned Browne and the last act of Jonathan Wild upon the gallows, and smiling a little sadly to myself, I pressed twopence into his hand and passed on.

INDEX

Abraham Men, 77–82

"Academy Buz-Nappers," 151

Aitkin, James, *alias* Hill, *alias* Hind, *alias* Jack the Painter, 218–220

Alazono-Mastix, 162

Albumazar, 23, 147

Alchemist, The, 108

Allen, the Highwayman, 209, 210

Almshouses, 55

"Alsatia," *see* Whitefriars.

Amends for Ladies, 180

Amusements Serious and Comical, 183

Anatomy of Abuses, 31, 33

Anatomy of Melancholy, The, 65

Annals of the Reformation, Strype's, 88

Anniseed-Water Robin, 186–187

Argotiers, 40, 70

Armin, Robert, 147

Artful Dodger, The, 157

Art of Living in London, The, 234

Ascham, Roger, 131, 172

Astrology, 24

Aubrey, John, 78, 187, 193

Autolycus, 14, 83, 84, 148

Awdeley, John, 44; on Abraham Men, 81; 137–138, 160, 161, 197

Babington, Gervase, Bp. of Worcester, 170

Bacon, Francis, 130

Banbury, 84

Barbers, cheats of, 229–230

Barbers of Drury Lane, Five, 187

Barclay, Alexander, 40–41, 73

Bardolph, 127

"Barnard's Law," 174–175

Bartendale, John, 105

Bartholomew Fair, 87, 147, 156–157

Bawdybaskets, 85, 196

Bear Gardens, 152

Beaumont and Fletcher, 50, 71, 77, 84–85, 180

Bedlam, *see* St. Mary Bethlehem

Bednall Green, 225

Beggars, Elizabethan, 25–26; increase of, 29–36; pamphlets on, 40–45; language of, 44, 66, 96–98; punishments of, 45–55; orders of, 58–85; numbers of, 87–88; ceremonies of, 91–93; kings of, 92–94; laws of, 92; haunts of, 94–96; decline of, 191–200

Beggars, Mediaeval, 19–26, 27, 29; brotherhoods of, 36–39; laws of, 37–38; orders of, 37–38

Beggars' Bush, 59, 71

Beggars' Opera, The, 222

Beggers Ape, The, 134

Belle (in *Lavengro*), 85

Belman of London, The, 91, 138

Belman's Second Night Walke, The, 58

"Bermuda," 182

Black Bess, 216

Black Bookes Messenger, The, 101, 143, 146, 149

Black Death, The, 27, 28

Black Dogge of Newgate, The, 49

Blackfriars, 153

"Black Guard, The," 193

Blake, Joseph, *alias* Blueskin, 236, 237

Blandy, Mary, 103

Blear-eyed Moll, 167

Blind Beggar of Bednall Green, The, 179

Blind Beggar, The, 159

Blood, Colonel, 223–224

"Blue Sue," 233

Bobadil, 61, 127, 180

Body-Snatchers, *see* Resurrection Men

Bonny, Anne, 113, 183

Borrow, George, 236
Bottomley, Bess, 85
Bounce, Stephen, 230
Bowels Opened, 137
Bow Street Runners, 221
Breton, Nicholas, 126, 156
Brewen, Mrs., 101
Bridewell, 55, 69–70, 155, 230
Bristol, 219, 220
British Museum, The, 117
Brome, Richard, 60, 76, 89
Browne, Ned, 100–101, 167, 197,
　243
Browne, Sir Thomas, 59
Brown, Thomas, 177, 183, 233
Bunyan, John, 192, 193, 242
Burbie, Cuthbert, 140
Burton, Robert, 65

"Cadator, The, 228
Canidia, or The Witches, 99, 160
Cant, Beggars', 44, 66, 96–98
Captain Booth, 167
Card-cheating, 168–170, 172–176,
　221–222
Carew, Bampfylde-Moore, 93, 94,
　195–199, 226
Carew, Sir Thomas, 198
Carlo Buffone, 134
Cavalrice, 166
Caveat for Common Curseters, Har-
　man's, 44–45, 50, 52, 67–70
Chambers, Arthur, 233
Character of a Coffee-House, 180
Charities, 34–35
Charles I, 188, 191, 192
Charles II, 187, 224
Charley Bates, 151
Chatham, 216
Chaucer, Geoffrey, 75, 83, 84
Cheapside, 50, 70
Cheaters Cheated, The, 149
Chelsea, 117
"Cheting Law, The," 171
Chettle, Henry, 24, 94, 143, 145,
　158

Chickley, Robert, 35
Chipping Norton, 209
Chosroes, King of the Beggars, 40
Christ's Hospital, 55
Christian Exercise, Parsons', 143
Christopher Catchpoll, 42
Clancie, Major, 192, 226–228
Clapperdudgeons, 38, 40–41, 67,
　70–74, 86, 197, 242
Clause Patch, 197
Clavell, John, 204, 206
"Clewners, The," 93
"Cloyer, The," 154
Cobbler of Canterbury, The, 142
Cock Alley, 236
Cock Lorell, 38–39, 84, 87
Cock Lorells Bote, 41–42, 43
Cold Harbour, 123
Collins, Philip, 103
Colonel Jack, 64, 225–226
Compleynt of Roderyck Mors, 31–32
Compters, *see* Prisons
Compters Commonwealth, The, 162
Conduit Street, 118
Coneys, *see* Gulls
Coneycatchers, 114, 120–122; in
　"Alsatia," 122; 124, 125; in
　Pauls' Walk, 126–129; 133, 134,
　135, 136–143, 145, 146; orders
　of, 146–164; Laws of, 165–176,
　228–233; 184, 185, 214, 215,
　221–239; watchwords of, 126,
　226; 234– 239
Coneycatching Pamphlets, 86,
　137–139
Copland, Robert, 43, 59, 63, 76,
　97
Coryat, Thomas, 130
Cottington, Jack, *alias* Mulled
　Sack, 186–187
Counterfeit Cranks, 67, 68, 69, 84,
　199
Coursours, The, 137
"Court of Miracles," 70
"Courtesy Man, The," 146, 160–
　162, 197, 227, 228

Cowley, Abraham, 117
Coxcomb, The, 77, 85
Cromwell, Oliver, 187
Crowder, the Highwayman, 207
Crowley, Robert, 30–31
Croydon, 173
Cunning Northerne Beggar, The, 72
"Curber's Law," 121, 166–167, 194, 230
Cuthbert Conny-Catcher, 142

"Dancing Doll," 233
Davies, W. H., 241
Davison, Frank, 83
Day, John, 179
Dead Tearme, The, 128
Deadman's Place, 122
Dedications, Elizabethan, 166
Defence of Conny-Catching, 139, 142
Defoe, Daniel, 52, 198, 234
Dekker, Thomas, 20, 52; on Gypsies, 56–58; 66, 72; on Abraham Men, 81–82; 88, 91, 95, 96, 97; on Elizabethan London, 119; on Paul's Walk, 127–128; on the Gulls, 133, 134, 138, 157; on Dicing, 171; 196
"Dells," 85
Deloney, Thomas, 113
Dennis, Thomas, 196
Description of England, Harrison's, 32, 53
Description of Love, A, 62
Der Betler Orden, 40
Deuville, Sir Gosseline, 21
Devil Tavern, 125, 183, 184, 186, 187, 212
de Veil, Colonel, 225
Diary of Henry Machyn, 153, 155
Diccon the Bedlam, 79
Dice Cosenage, The, 38, 168–172
Dick Swiveller, 230
Dickenson, John, 142, 143, 144
Diets Dry Dinner, 178
Diogines Lanthorne, 120–121
Discoveries of John Poulter, 203, 229

Discoverie of Witchcrafte, 24
Disputation, Greene's, 86, 143, 155
Diver, Jenny (Mary Young), 233
Dixon, Robert, 99, 160
Doctor Pinchbacke, 24
Dol Common, 108
Dona Britannica Hollandia, 123–124
Don Quixote, 148
"Doxies," 85, 196
"Drawlatches," 20–21
Drunken Barnaby, 173
Duchess of Malfy, The, 79
Duck Lane, 110
Duke Humphrey's Walk, 148
"Dummerers," 77
Dun House Tavern, 235
Durrest Fair, 95, 96
Du Vall, Claude, 207–208

Eagle Inn, 112
Earle, John, 127–128
Edgeworth the Foist, 147, 156–157
Edward VI, 46, 54
Edwards, Talbot, 223–224
Egerton Papers, The, 104
Eliot, Dr., 202
Elizabeth, Queen, 46, 55, 75, 153, 173
Ellis, Jack, 153
Ellwood, Thomas, 52
Enclosures, 29–32
English Gusman, The, 211
English Rogue, The, 57–58, 193–195
Epping Forest, 217, 218
Evelyn, John, 78
Everett, John, 207, 208
Every Man in His Humour, 132
Every Man Out of His Humour, 134

Fair Quarrel, A, 179
Fairfax, Lady, 153–154
Fairs, 148–150
"Falconers," 166
Falstaff, 61, 127, 152, 158, 169, 180

"Faungest, The," 161, 165
"Fawney Rig," The, 229
Fennor, William, 138, 159, 162
Field, Nathaniel, 180
Field, William, 236
Fielding, Henry, 221, 225, 237–238
"Figging Law," The, 147, 151
Filcher, the Foist, 149–150
"Filchmans," 66
Finch, Margaret, 93
Fish, Simon, 42
"Five Jumps at Leapfrog," 165
Fleet Street, 185, 188, 212
Fleetwood, William, 46
Foists, 70, 146–160, 171, 185, 186, 187, 204, 233
"Footman's Maund," 71
Fortunate Isles, The, 112
Fortunes of Nigel, The, 122, 125
Foure Letters, 141, 144
Foure PP, The, 84
Franklin, John, 103–104
Fraternitye of Vacaboundes, The, 44, 160, 161
"Fraters," The, 75
Frith, Mary (Moll Cutpurse), 183–188, 208, 222–223
Fulham, 171
Fuller, Thomas, 30, 73, 114, 166, 183

Gammer Gurton's Nedle, 79
Genings, Nicholas, 14, 67–70
Gentle Crafte, The, 113
George II, 222
Gerbier, Sir Balthazar, 53–54
"Glimmering Morts," 85
Globe Tavern, 185
Goadby, Mrs., 199
Goodman, Nicholas, 123
Gosson, Stephen, 152
Greene, Robert, 86, 88; on Ned Browne, 100–101; 138, 139–145, 146, 147, 154–155, 165, 175, 215
Greene's Tu Quoque, 169

Gregg, John, 192
Gregory the Hangman, 154
Greyfriars, 55
Guilds, Decay of, 35–36
Guilpin, Edward, 128
Gulls, The, 32–33, 120, 128, 129–135; "Twelvepenny Gulls," 133; at the theatre, 134; 136, 160, 161, 162, 165, 168–176
"Gull-Gropers," 171
Guls Hornebook, The, 133–134
Guy of Warwick, 23
Gyffon, James, 47
Gypsies, 19, 56–58, 93
Gypsies Metamorphosed, The, 76
"Half-Hanged Smith," 104
Halifax, Guillotine at, 53
Hall, Jack, 230
Hall, Joseph, 135
Hamlet, 132
Harman, Thomas, 44–45, 50, 52; on Gypsies, 57; on Genings, 67–70; 85, 86, 95, 138, 233
Harrison, William, 32, 53, 87
Harvey, Gabriel, 112, 141, 144, 145
Hatton Gardens, 215
Hayman, Robert, 127
Head, Richard, 193
"Heavers," 165
Hemings, Edward, 191
Henry VII, 45
Henry VIII, 42, 45, 111, 112
Hertford, Lady, 202
Hext, Edward, 49, 88, 95
Heywood, John, 84
"High Huffers," 178
Highwayman on Foot, The, 38
Highwaymen, 183, 201–203; haunts of, 204; laws of, 204–205; 206–220
Hind, James, 183, 208–213, 217
History of the Church, Thomas Fuller's, 166
Hitchcocke, Robert, 29
Hitchin, Charles, 236–237
Hodges, an ironmonger, 163–164

Holinshed, Raphael, 54–55
Holland's Leaguer, 123–124
Hollands Leaguer (Goodman), 123, 124
Holland's Leaguer (Marmion), 124
Holy and Prophane State, The, 30
Honest Man's Fortune, The, 180
"Hookers," 167
Horsey, Samuel, 93
Hospitals, Closing of, 36
Hounslow Heath, 202, 204
Houses of Correction, 46, 49, 52, 55, 73
Howell, James, 131
Howleglass, 23
Hue and Cry, 47, 206
Hugo, Victor, 70, 151
Hull, Sarah, 233
Humphrey, Duke of Gloucester, 127
Humphry Clinker, 202
Hunter, John, 233
Huon of Bordeaux, 23
Hutton, Luke, 49, 104–105
Hye Way to the Spitel Hous, 43, 63

Inns of Court, 191
Instructions for Forreine Travell, 131
Isam, Mistress, 143
Islington, 46, 117
Italianate Englishmen, 131–132

Jack the Painter, *see* Aitkin, James
"Jacks of the Clock House," 166
Jackson the Highwayman, 207, 213–216
Jackson's Recantation, 208, 213, 215
Jacob Hildebrod, 122
Jacob's Well, 21
James I, 55, 156, 178, 191, 209
"Jarkemen," 75
Jenkin Cowdiddle, 37
"Jibber the Kibber," 232
Johnson, Samuel, 118, 166
Jonson, Ben, 76, 108, 112, 125, 156–157

Joviall Crew, A, 60, 76
Justice Overdo, 147

Kempe, William, 155
"Ken-Miller," The, 206
Kidd, Captain, 216
"Kinchin Coves," 77, 206
Kind Heartes Dreame, 145
King, Thomas, 208, 217–218
King Henry VI, pt. ii, 73–74
King Lear, 130
"King's Takers," 165
"Kinning by the Parapet," 230
"Klenckners," 72
"Knights of the Post," 157–158
Knowls, Thomas, 212

Lamb, Charles, 191, 199
Lambeth Marshes, 119
Langland, William, 20, 21, 78
Latrucino, 148
Lavengro, 85, 241
Lemmon, Obadiah, 235
Lewkenor's Lane, 150–151, 196–197
Liber Vagatorum, 49, 67, 72
Life and Adventures of Moore Carew, 92, 197–198
Life and Death of Gamaliel Ratsey, 106
Life and Death of Mrs. Mary Frith, 184
Life and Death of William Longbeard, 22
"Lifting Law," 165, 229
Lincoln's Inn Fields, 94, 95
"Little Snakesman," 206
London, 117–129
London Bridge, 117
London and the Country Carbonadoed, 78
London Spy, The, 122
London's Ordinary, 124–125
Long Acre, 233
Longbeard, William, 22
Long Lawrence, 38

Long Meg of Westminster, 110, 111–114, 179, 183
Look on me, London, 172
Lord Dalgarno, 122, 125
Lord Feesimple, 180
Lord Glenvarloch, 122, 125
Loving Mad Tom, 72
Low, Richard, 230
Luke Hutton's Repentance, 105
Lupton, Donald, 78
Luther, Martin, 40, 163

Macaulay, Lord, 121–122
Macheath, 222
Machyn, Henry, 153, 155
Mahoney, J., 104
Maidenhead Thicket, 215
Maintenance, 29
Mamillia, 141
Man of Feeling, The, 199–200
Manifest Detection of Dice-Play, 169, 171–172
Market Deeping, 105, 106
Markham, G., 166
Marlborough Downs, 213, 215
Marlowe, Christopher, 140, 141
Marmion, Shakerley, 124
Marriage of the Arts, 178
Marston, John, 134
"Martin," The, 206
Martin Mark-all, 74, 138
Marylebone, 117
"Mason's Maund," 71
Master-Thief Discovered, The, 212
Master-Wardens, 93
Matthew Mumchance, 42
Matthews, Christopher, 235
Matthews, William, 235
Mendall, Jack, 37
Meriton Latroon, 57–58, 71, 94, 193–195, 209, 210, 226
Mermaid Tavern, 124, 125
Middleton, Thomas, 56, 131–132, 148, 179, 183
Mihil Mumchance, 138
Milliner, Mary, 236

Mitre Tavern, 124
Moll Cutpurse, *see* Frith, Mary
Monasteries, Dissolution of, 35–36
Moorditch, 158
More, Sir Thomas, 30; on Fish's Pamphlet, 42
"Morning Sneaks," 230
Mr. Badman, 193, 194
Mr. Sponge, 228
Mr. Wiseman, 102
Murphy, Ann, 233
Musgrave, John, 34
Mynshul, Geoffrey, 49–50

Nan, the Foist, 86, 143, 154–155
Nashe, Thomas, 33, 141
Naturall and Artificiall Directions, 178
Nell's Ordinary, 227
Nevison, the Highwayman, 203
Newark, 156
Newgate, 49–50, 103, 110, 186, 212, 213, 227, 233
New Mad Tom of Bedlam, 80
Nightingale, the Nip, 156–157
Nim, the Foist, 149–150
"Nips," 70, 146–160, 204, 229
Nixon, Antony, 138, 160
Northbrooke, J., 168, 171, 173
Notable Discovery of Coosnage, A, 139, 175
Notre Dame, 70
Nut-Brown Maid, The, 25

O per se O, 52, 72, 81–82
Orange Dicers, 228–229
Ordinaries, 125–126, 170
Osric, in *Hamlet*, 132
Overbury, Sir Thomas, 84

Palliards, *see* Clapperdudgeons
Pandosto, 141
Pardoner, Chaucer's, 75
Parker, George, 77, 232
Partridge, 207
Parson's Tale, 32
Pasquils Passe & Passeth Not, 126

Patrico, 65–66, 75–76
Paul's Cross, 186
Paul's Walk, 126–129, 133–135,
    148
Pedlars, 82–84
Pedlar's French, see Cant
Peele, George, 140, 141
Phillipps, Thomas, 53, 208, 236
Pickering, Lawrence, 86, 142–143
Picthatch, 70
Piers Plowman, 20–21
Pillory, 50, 51, 70, 152
Pirates, 90–91
Plymouth, 219
Pollitique Platt, A., 29
Portsmouth, 219
Poulter, John, 229
Pressing to Plead, 53
"Priggers of Prancers," 77
Prisons, 48–50
Privy Search, The, 48
Puddle Wharf, 121
"Puffing Dick," 37–38

"Quartern of Knaves," The, 38
"Queer Plungers," 231
Quodlibets, 127

Radcliffe, Ralph, 129
Ratsbuch, 40
Ratsey, Gamaliel, 89, 105–111
Ratsey's Repentance, 105
Read, Mary, 113
Reading, 215
Recantation of an Ill-Led Life, 204,
    206
Receivers, 235, 236
Redman, Bishop, 35
Regulator, The, 231, 233, 236–237
Repentance of Robert Greene, 102, 140,
    143–144
Resurrection Men, 218, 232–233
Reynard the Fox, 22, 89
Rhodes, Jack, 100, 154
Richard II, 45
"Ring Fallers," 163–164, 176, 229

"Ringing Tuggs," 229
Roaring Boys, 122, 132–133, 177–
    188
Roaring Girle, The, 66, 183
Roberdes Men, 20–21, 37
Roberts, King of the Beggars, 37
Robert the Devil, 22
Robin Hood, 21
Rogues' Calendar, The, 230
Ronco, 147
Rookwood, 216
Rowlands, Samuel, 52; on Ruff-
    lers, 61, 62; 74, 96, 120–121,
    138, 175, 215
"Rowlipolly," 228
Roxburghe Ballads, 50, 173, 182
"Royal Scamps," 207, 208
"Rufflers," 28, 38, 60–63, 66, 67,
    71, 86, 100, 121
Rugosa, 23
"Rum-Snoosers," 231
"Rutter," The, 174, 176

Sadler, Thomas, 223
St. Bartholomew's Church, 59
St. Bartholomew's Hospital, 36, 55
St. Dunstan's Church, 152
St. Giles, 118
St. Mary Bethlehem, 36, 78–79
St. Mary Overy, 225–226
St. Paul's Cathedral, 117, 120,
    126–129, 133, 148, 166, 168
St. Sepulchre, 52
St. Thomas of Southwark, 36, 55
Satires, Hall's, 178
Scot, Reginald, 24, 173–174
Scott, Sir Walter, 122, 125, 178–179
Scourge of Corruption, The, 160
"Scupper," The, 206
Sermon in Praise of Thieves, 76
Serving Men, 33–35
Shadwell, Thomas, 132–133
Shakespeare, William, 73–74, 83,
    141, 147
Sheppard, Jack, 192, 236
Shift, 160

Ship of Fools, Barclay's, 40–41, 43, 73
Shirley, John, 167
Shooter's Hill, 209, 210
Shorthouse, 109
Shotover Hill, 212
Sibbes, Dr., 136–137
Simpcox, 73–74
Siquila, 170
Sir Oliver Anchovy, 160
Skelton, King of the Beggars, 38
Skialethia, 128
Smart's Quay, 150
Smith, John, *alias* Buckhorse, 197
Snell, 109, 110
"Snudge," The, 167
Society for the Reformation of Manners, 55
Sogliardo, 134
Solomon, King of the Beggars, 93
Song of a Constable, 47
Song of Solomon, The, 136
Southward, 123
Spalding, 106
Spanish Gypsy, The, 56
Spiggot, William, 208, 236
Spising, King of the Beggars, 37
Squire of Alsatia, The, 132–133
Stamford, 84
Statute of Labourers, 45
Stephens, John, 130
Stephen, the Gull, 132
Sterne, Laurence, 232
Stocks, The, 44, 45, 50
Stourton, Lord Charles, 82
Stout Cripple of Cornwall, 73
Stradling, John, 44–45, 82
Strype, John, 55, 87, 88
Stubbes, Philip, 31; on extravagance in dress, 33; on apprentices, 36; 52, 179
Sumptuary Laws, 33
Supplicacyon for the Beggers, 42
Surveyor of Vagrants, 55
"Sweetner's Law," 228
Swift, Dick, 235

Swift, Jonathan, 104
"Swygmen," *see* Pedlars
Sykes, James ("Hell and Fury"), 236

"Taker-Up," The, 174–175
"Tattogeys," 228
Taverns, 124–126
Taylor, John, 62, 155, 159
Tearcat, 66
Testament of James Hynd, 183, 213
Tewkesbury, Battle of, 37
Thames, 117–118
Thief-Catcher, The, 203–204, 222
Thief Takers, 234–235, 237
"Thimble-Rig," The, 221–222
Three Tuns, The, 124
"Tickers," 230
Tinkers, 83, 84–85
Tobacco, 177–178
"Tolliban Rig," The, 77.
Tom a Bedlam, *see* Abraham Men
Tom Jones, 56, 207
Tom of Lincoln, 23
Tottenham Court Road, 232
Treatise Against Dicing, etc., 168, 171, 173
Trincalo, 147
Triumph of Wit, 23, 167
Triumph of London, The, 131
Turnmill Street, 70
Turpin, Richard, 207, 208, 216–218
Tyburn, 52–53, 64, 104, 155, 159, 213, 223, 228, 233, 238
Tyler, Wat, 27

Underhill, Edward, 172
Unemployment, 28–29
"Upright Men," 38, 63–67, 68, 69, 76, 91, 92
Utopia, More's, 30

"Verser," The, 174–175
View of Society and Manners, 232
Villon, François, 222

Walker, Gilbert, 168–169, 171–172
Walker, the Foist, 153–154
Walpole, Horace, 202
Walton, Izaak, 83, 94
Ward, Ned, 49, 50, 78–79, 122
Watchmen, 47
Water Lane, 122
Wat Welbelyne, 42
Wealth, a cause of beggary, 32–33
"Whip-Jacks," 74–75, 197
Whipping at the cart's tail, 50–52
Whitefriars, 36, 67, 70–71, 94, 121–123, 158, 179, 182, 225

Whitney, James, 208
Widow, The, 148
Wild, Jonathan, 184, 185, 232, 234–238, 243
"Wiltners," The, 163
Winter's Tale, 83, 148
Wood, Antony, 54
Wood Street Compter, 235–236
Wordsworth, Dorothy, 75, 241
Work for Chimney-Sweepers, 178
Wyll of the Devyll, 43–44

Young, Mary, *see* Diver, Jenny

GEORGE ALLEN & UNWIN LTD
LONDON: 40 MUSEUM STREET, W.C.1
LEIPZIG: (F. VOLCKMAR) HOSPITALSTR. 10
CAPE TOWN: 73 ST. GEORGE'S STREET
TORONTO: 91 WELLINGTON STREET, WEST
BOMBAY: 15 GRAHAM ROAD, BALLARD ESTATE
WELLINGTON, N.Z.: 8 KINGS CRESCENT, LOWER HUTT
SYDNEY, N.S.W.: AUSTRALIA HOUSE, WYNYARD SQUARE

Those Were Good Days

by CARL LUDWIG SCHLEICH

TRANSLATED BY BERNARD MIALL

Demy 8vo. *Illustrated* 12s 6d. net

The reminiscences of Carl Ludwig Schleich, a distinguished if somewhat heretical surgeon and pathologist, and the pioneer of local anaesthesia, who was also a brilliant musician and painter, and a writer of great originality, should make interesting and unusual reading. Schleich was the intimate friend of Strindberg, to whom he devotes a revealing chapter, the pupil and assistant of the great Virchow, and a friend of Paul Ehrlich. A Pomeranian, the son of a Stettin physician, of whom he paints an unforgettable picture, Schleich was a true citizen of the "old Germany" of poets, musicians, philosophers, and scientists, which has always enjoyed the respect and affection of the civilized world; but there was something individual, irrepressible, and lawless in this little Pomeranian surgeon which will endear him to English readers. His autobiography contains a delightful record of a happy and untrammelled childhood, a description of riotous rather than studious years at several universities, the history of an unusual and somewhat troubled career, and a number of valuable portraits of men whose names are household words.

Brahms: His Life and Work

by KARL GEIRINGER

Demy 8vo. *Illustrated* 12s. 6d. net

Since the appearance of the last biography of Johannes Brahms, much new and important material concerning him has become available. In the archives of Viennese Society of the Friends of Music, Dr. Geiringer has discovered more than a thousand letters written by Brahms or addressed to him, and held hitherto under legal seal, and the new biography is enriched by letters of Brahms's parents and eminent contemporaries such as Robert and Clara Schumann, Anton Dvorak, Sir George Grove, Sir George Henschel, Mathilde Wesendonk, and others. This extensive material inevitably throws fresh and important light upon Brahms's character and the events of his life, and no less upon the persons with whom his life was bound up. The author has also had access to many original manuscripts and printed copies in which Brahms himself inserted corrections, which have not so far been used by biographers.

John Nash

Architect to King George IV

by JOHN SUMMERSON

Demy 8vo. *Illustrated* 10s. 6d. net

The remarkable career of John Nash, architect and adventurer, has never hitherto been explored, although he is one of the few English architects whose lives, apart from purely professional activities, are worth recording. Mr. Summerson's book, in breaking this new ground, combines a critical account of Nash's architecture and town-planning with the story of his life. The building of Regent Street and Regent's Park is described in detail, and separate chapters are devoted to the Pavilion at Brighton and Buckingham Palace. All these, as well as Nash's numerous country houses (many hitherto unrecorded), are illustrated from drawings, prints and photographs.

Zaharoff, the Armaments King
by ROBERT NEUMANN
TRANSLATED BY R. T. CLARK

Demy 8vo.   10s. 6d. net

Sir Basil Zaharoff is still one of the mystery men of Europe. Was he a mere unscrupulous adventurer, a modern pirate, a humble member of a formidable conspiracy against the peace of Europe or a high-souled patriot using what instruments offered him for the benefit of his country? And if so what country? Is this member of the British Knightage a Greek, Jew, or Roumanian? Was what he was credited with doing his own work or was he a tool of secret interests? What, in fact, did he do and is he doing? Herr Robert Neumann has persistently tracked down every ascertainable fact and, so far as the investigator can, stripped the falsehood away. The result is to lose some of the mystery and gain more, because under the investigator's microscope Zaharoff seems a greater enigma than ever. This is a work which has all the characteristics of the best type of detective story, and at the same time it is, especially in these days of arms traffic scandals, a contribution to recent history which the serious student cannot neglect.

Emil Ludwig has said: "Neumann's book is an indictment at a high level. . . . I only regret that it is not given away for all to read."

Edison
HIS LIFE, HIS WORK, HIS GENIUS
by WILLIAM ADAMS SIMONDS

Demy 8vo.   *Illustrated*   10s. 6d. net

Edison's name evokes a sense of wizardry, an impression of fabulous achievement, a suggestion of alchemy and magic. Here is a true picture of the man, as he began and as he became; the influences and impulses rooted in childhood; his work an unparalleled record of the devotion and absorption; and his genius made understandable, as nearly understandable as genius can be made, expressed in terms of human needs, compounded of dreams, of imagination, of infinite patience.

Edison's own notebooks, his papers, and his letters have been searched. Members of the family were consulted. His co-workers and associates were called on for help. Visits were made to the scenes of his life, and so much new material has been made available and incorporated into this biography. Technically accurate, though non-technical in style, this book presents a richly coloured portrait of an extraordinary man, and is in addition a true reflection of the America of his time.

My Seven Selves
by HAMILTON FYFE
Author of *Northcliffe, T. P. O'Connor*, etc.

Demy 8vo.   *Illustrated*   12s. 6d. net

Mr. Hamilton Fyfe has based his autobiography on an interesting idea. If the substance of our bodies were not in perpetual change we should stagnate and die. Mr. Hamilton Fyfe holds that the same process must go on in all minds that are really alive, and that not to "change one's mind" from time to time is a symptom of mental stagnation. He illustrates this in his own case by tracing the seven different persons he has been since he began to possess a personality at all—the Foolish Young Fellow, the Fortunate Young Man, the Adventurer, the Looker-on, the Reformer, the Dupe, and finally a man purged of illusions "poor and content."

With a lively pen he describes the events of his varied and often exciting career as editor, star reporter, as war correspondent, and as world traveller. His story, vividly and frankly told, keeps an unfailing grip upon the reader's interest.

LONDON: GEORGE ALLEN & UNWIN, LTD.

198